content and organization of speeches

14- 120- 871

Speech Communication Series

content and organization of speeches

Walter F. Terris
Eastern Montana College

WM. C. BROWN COMPANY PUBLISHERS, *Dubuque, Iowa*

Speech Series

Consulting Editor
Baxter M. Geeting
Sacramento State College
Sacramento, California

Copyright © 1968 by
Wm. C. Brown Company Publishers

Library of Congress Catalog Card Number: 68–24359

ISBN 0–697–04108–5

Third Printing, 1970

Printed in the United States of America

Dynamic developments of our time, particularly the communication explosion and new revelations concerning human behavior, demand fresh approaches to the teaching of speech. Modern life places an emphasis on speech as an *act of communication*, interdisciplinary in nature, capable of adding new dimensions to man's evolution and progress in all areas of life. The SPEECH COMMUNICATION SERIES, addressed to the introductory student, represents a significant attempt to provide new materials for today's teaching needs.

Basic to all titles in the series is the desire to present the material in the clearest and most lucid style for the purpose of making speech communication a useful, ethical and satisfying experience. While the individual titles are self-contained, collectively they provide the substance for a comprehensive study of those topics fundamental to a basic course in speech communication.

PREFACE

Some students will be completely satisfied with their instructor's simple, authoritarian assertion that *this* is the way you prepare a speech. The teacher tells him how and the student does it. If the student is mature and intelligent, however, he will want to know why.

The mechanical minutiae of putting together a readable outline, preparing a set of note cards, or developing specific techniques of practice and delivery are best taught by some form of practical experience. Let the student try to perform the tasks listed above and then criticize them constructively.

This book is an attempt to discover some reasons *why* a speech is put together the way it is. It tries to explore the alternatives open to the speaker when he approaches the problems and the choices involved in communicating his ideas. The book confronts these choices in the order in which the speaker himself is likely to face them. It tries to treat each choice with sufficient depth so that the speaker will at least be aware of the magnitude of his difficulties and the range of his choices.

I have a great thanks for two of my colleagues at the University of Denver. The figures in this book are the work of Alton Barbour. The typing was done in friendship and without compensation by Mrs. Evelyn Sieburg. I appreciate the friendship more than I can say.

CONTENTS

Chapter 1

AN INTRODUCTORY VIEWPOINT: STEREOTYPE AND CHANGE

This book deals with the public speech. It distinguishes this form of address from other forms such as group discussion, conversation, and dialogue. The latter are less formal, more spontaneous. The public speech is stereotyped by the upright (and often rigid) speaker pontificating before rows of listeners. This stereotype causes the speaker's biggest problem. The supposed formality and rigidity of the public speaking situation makes the speaker seem like a different animal from the person he is in normal conversation. It needn't. The situations are not that different.

All public speaking and all conversation are simply specific forms of communication. The diagram below gives an idealized picture of the basic elements of the communication situation.

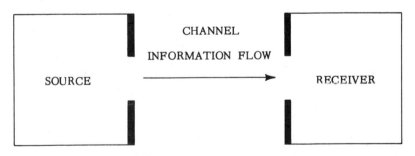

Figure 1

This diagram tends to be inclusive, not definitive. Depending on the viewpoint of the person making the definition, communication is defined as part or all of the elements in the diagram. Some researchers in the field of communication are interested only in the capacity of the channel over which messages are sent. Some are concerned with the nature of information. Some insist that the source of information must be human and must transmit symbols intentionally, while others believe that physical-energy transfers from objects, if received and interpreted by humans, should also be called communication. Some communication theorists limit communication to the generation of meaning; that is, they consider to be communication any meaning that the receiver makes out of his world.

Under most circumstances communication is a two-way process.

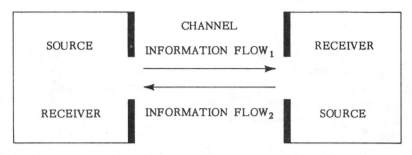

Figure 2

If the system diagrammed above is considered primarily from the point of view of the first source at the left, then the return information flow (Information Flow$_2$) is sometimes known as feedback.

In the public speech, the object of our concern here, all of these elements are present. There is, however, one additional element: an intent on the part of the source to bring about some change in a human receiver by means of the information transmitted. Put another way, the public speech is always a persuasive situation. If there is no intent to change an audience in some way, the public speech has no meaning.

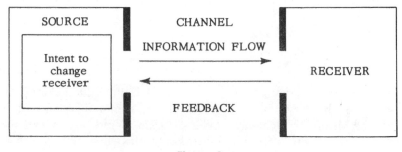

Figure 3

Even in situations where the speaker himself would say that he has no such intention, the intent must be present. If the speaker says that he simply wanted to inform his audience, then it must certainly follow that he intended the audience to be more informed, more knowledgeable at the end of the speech than they were at its beginning. They will have, at least, a greater store of information. And it is the rare speaker who does not feel that the audience will be better for having received the information.

The entertainer wants an even more drastic change. He wants an overt change in physical response: applause, laughter, cheers.

The speaker may best be understood, then, as an agent of change. If he does not see himself at least potentially as such an agent of change in the specific situation he should avoid speaking at all cost. The speaker must determine, before speaking, how he can bring about change and a strategy for doing it.

It follows, then, that the speech is the instrument by which the intent to bring about change is carried out. It is the particular tactic executed within the strategy of change.

A WORD ABOUT THE STEREOTYPE

Someone might say that this definition of the public speech does not fit the stereotype described before. You're right, it doesn't. This could just as easily define the situation that exists in a casual conversation when one party to the conversation suddenly realizes that he wants the other party to change. From that point on, what the conversationalist says and does is part of a strategy for change. His procedure, then, though perhaps he does not realize it, is essentially the same as the procedure of the politician in a campaign, the travelogue lecturer, or the teacher in a classroom. The only difference comes in nonessentials: whether the audience and the speaker sit or stand, the number in the audience, the physical conditions in the room, the opportunity for audience response, the length and formality of the message, the nature of the channel. Undoubtedly all these factors influence the strategy, but the essential character of that strategy is unchanged.

It is generally the formality of the speaking situation that frightens the first-time speaker. The same person who speaks with real feeling and animation over coffee in the Student Union, somehow becomes an inanimate creature with a ramrod for a spine when he is faced with making a formal public speech. He no longer has the security of talking to a single individual, and suddenly the audience becomes an amorphous mass that seems both bored and hostile.

There is a solution to this problem. Treat every audience as a col-
lection of distinct individuals. Talk to people, not audiences. Does this
sound simple? It is, and it is infallibly effective. We will return to this
solution before we finish.

THE NATURE OF STRATEGY

If the speaker really wants the listener to change, he has three major
areas, and perhaps a fourth, of concern. The first is the definition of
the specific change he intends; the second is an analysis of some of the
factors within the listener that determine change; the third is the nature
of the message he constructs; and the fourth is the moral limitation he
places upon himself.

DETERMINING THE INTENDED CHANGE

What do you believe and what does the listener believe? Where does
he stand on the issues involved and where do you stand? How do you
feel about the issues and how does he feel? When you have answered
these questions then you must state what you want him to believe,
how you want him to feel, where you want him to be, and what you
want him to do. The speaker must determine precisely the response he
wants from his listener, if for no other reason than to be able to know
when he fails.

The ability to answer these questions will depend upon the speaker's
ability to describe accurately both himself and his listener. The speaker
must determine in advance the listeners' predispositions, attitudes, moods,
and feelings. Then he must determine how they differ from his own. The
speaker must determine how far the listener is capable of changing and
then he must be able to state the change he intends clearly and spe-
cifically.

This process of measuring the differences, at least the differences
that matter, between the listener and the speaker will not only determine
how the latter goes about preparing his speech but also how he gives
it and alters it from moment to moment. The speaker, even while he is
speaking, should have an awareness of how his listener expresses his
attitudes and feelings. He then must be able to monitor these responses
and adjust the speech accordingly.

THE FACTORS OF CHANGE

There is no way of determining in advance what will make a particular person change or, even what made the change after it has oc-

curred. Even the person himself often cannot tell you why he changed. What we do have available are psychological generalizations which describe how large groups of people tend to act in particular situations or how specific people have acted in carefully controlled laboratory situations. The chances are very great that a particular listener will not act as the textbook says he should.

THE STRUCTURE OF THE MESSAGE

The message, when it finally comes out, should take into consideration the speaker's analysis of himself and his audience, the definition of the change he intends to stimulate, and his best understanding of what might best dispose the listener to change. If he has done all this carefully, he may or may not get the response he wanted. A perfect response will almost never be achieved. What the message meant to the speaker will never be more than an approximation of its meaning to the listener. In fact, the probability is very great that the speaker's ideas will be different from the ideas generated in the listener.

Communicating is a chancy business. There is even the chance that the speaker may achieve his ends without spending a moment's thought on preparation. In a particular situation he may be better off if he just plunges ahead. Over the long haul, however, the speaker is probably consistently more effective if he considers the factors which this book will talk about. Perhaps most important, the speaker will more accurately be able to tell when he fails to achieve his ends and will be able to analyze the causes of his failure. He may then be able to improve his next performance.

Conscious attention to speech preparation has another benefit. If one does not prepare his speech carefully it is likely that, whether he fails or succeeds, he won't know precisely what he did. This book contends that there are some things that the speaker has no moral warrant to do. If the speaker knows what he is doing he can more effectively fulfill his moral responsibilities as an agent of change.

ETHICS AND THE SPEAKER

This book has a particular ethical viewpoint that will be made clear later. It is very easy for the speaker to approach a listener as a person who needs changing. If the speaker feels strongly about making that change and if the rewards to the speaker for successfully changing the listener are great, there is strong motivation for the speaker to treat the listener like an object. The speaker may view the listener as someone to manipulate, someone to deceive, or pressure, into changing. The moment he does that he has violated the listener and, worse yet, violated himself.

When a listener consents to hear a speech he gives the speaker a position of potential influence. There may then be a predisposition on the part of the listener to change in the direction that the speaker intends. When a speaker has been granted a platform he has been granted a discretionary power. The first amendment to the Constitution guarantees the speaker's freedom but it does not mention any responsibility on his part. That responsibility is determined by each speaker in each situation. It is an individual decision that each speaker makes.

A JUDGMENT

The construction of a public speech is one long series of choices, none of them easy. The speaker is faced with choices about the audience and himself. He must choose to attempt change. He must choose a strategy for change. He makes choices throughout the construction of his message. At every point he commits himself to an ethical dilemma and at each point he demonstrates to his listener what sort of person he is. He is judged at every choice and he is safe from this judgment nowhere.

EXERCISES

1. Discuss what things you would add to the model of communication in Figure I.
2. Describe the kind of speech course you would construct based on the ideas expressed in this chapter.

READINGS

On the nature of communication, see:

LaRusso, Dominick, *Basic Skills of Oral Communication* (Dubuque: Wm. C. Brown Company Publishers, 1967), pp. 1-27.

Weaver, Carl H., and Warren L. Strausbaugh, *Fundamentals of Speech Communication* (New York: American Book Company, 1964), pp. 3-68.

On communication as persuasion, see:

Campbell, James H., and Hal W. Hepler, "Persuasion and Interpersonal Relations," in *Dimensions of Communication* (Belmont, California: Wadsworth Publishing Company, 1965), pp. 87-95.

Chapter 2

DETERMINING
THE INTENDED CHANGE

The first step in speech preparation is taken in the speaker's mind. What do I want to talk about? Many times the situation will dictate the subject. The report to be given in class is seldom a free choice, just as particular issues to be dealt with in a political campaign are seldom the choice of the candidate. The general rule to follow is simple. Choose only those subjects you care about. If you don't care, don't speak.

You have to care about both the subject and the listener. You have to care about the change you intend to stimulate in the listener. You have to care about the consequences of that change. If you do not really care about any one of these elements, your listener soon knows it. Few listeners are so naive that they cannot spot a phony when they hear one.

CHOOSING THE SUBJECT

The following questions may lead you to a proper choice of subject.

1. *What does the situation call for?*

When a speaker gives a speech, the subject is determined generally by the people who ask him to speak, either tacitly or explicitly. The Kiwanis Club knows you are a student of the life of Sir Winston Churchill and is interested in knowing more about this statesman—you will not talk about the life cycle of the emperor moth. If you are an expert in the field of the genetic effects of radiation and you have been asked to speak at a Ban-the-Bomb meeting, you do not speak about the use of radio-active isotopes as tracers. You have publicly expressed yourself on the question of the freedom of expression as it relates to pornography and obscenity, and the Committee for Decent Literature has grudgingly given you fifteen minutes to "express your radical ideas"—you do not waste their time and yours with a book review.

If you are asked to speak, the people asking thought you knew about something they were interested in. You then have the obligation to stick within their reasonable limits. Of course your feelings have something to do with the choice. Wendell Phillips, the nineteenth-century American abolitionist, offered to speak on his usual topic, "The Liberal Arts," for his usual fee but if the sponsoring organization allowed him to talk about the abolition of slavery he charged no fee. That is your option, too, but remember that listeners tend to be highly intolerant of how you use their time. You may speak about things important to you, but the ultimate choice is the audience's, for if they feel you are imposing on them, they will turn you off mentally just as quickly and just as effectively as they would turn off an obnoxious television commercial.

Most situations have a context within which a speaker must operate. A special lecture series, a foreign affairs discussion group, a convention of insurance underwriters: each of these situations naturally calls for a particular kind of subject. It is the rare speaker who is allowed to violate the restrictions imposed by the context. If you are the President of the United States and are invited to a Yale commencement, you can propose a plan for Latin American rapproachement. If you are the Prime Minister of England you can propose an alliance of the English-speaking peoples. The people reading this book, however, are not likely to fall into that category of speaker upon whom the context places no obligations.

In the context of a university classroom, even where your instructor gives you the widest latitude, you are not entirely free of contextual pressure. Even in the class where your primary object is learning to communicate, you may not ignore the situational rules. For instance:

a. You must offer something to the listener. It may be new information, a new interpretation, a different viewpoint, a new feeling. Anything less is a waste of time for you and for him. The deadliest type of speech is the "How to . . ." speech when the listener already knows how.

b. What you say must have significance for the listener. It must be either a subject with inherent importance to him or one which you can make important to him. The color of the fruit-fly's eyes may be the most interesting thing in the world to you, but unless it can be made significant for the listener it would be better to avoid the fruit-fly's eyes. Remember, however, that if you find a subject fascinating there must be reasons for that fascination. Find the reasons and maybe you can win a convert to your interest.

c. You must not bore your listener. No matter how new or important the information is, if you do not show a lively interest in the subject, it is not likely that your listener will find it interesting. Most of us have a tendency to soften our feelings about our ideas. If we get too tied up in an idea, show too much feeling for it, we lose face when that idea is criticized. There is a tendency, then, for the beginning speaker to appear uncommitted, even unconcerned about an idea. By doing this he feels he is protecting himself from being hurt by his listener. The boring speaker is often the frightened speaker. He may feel strongly about his subject, but he is too afraid of being hurt to show this. In the end this reticence is self-defeating. The listener rightly feels that if the speaker is not even interested in the subject, there is nothing interesting in it for him.

Thus even in the classroom learning experience there are some strictures on the selection of a topic.

2. *What am I capable of doing?*

An inability to speak on a particular subject may arise from several sources. The most obvious, yet usually the least important, difficulty arises from having too little information. Indeed, I would have difficulty talking to a convention of high-energy particle physicists on a subject in their own field, and though research on my part might narrow the gap between our relative stores of information, only years of study could give me a reasonable chance of making a meaningful speech to them. The gap in knowledge between the speaker and the listener is seldom this wide and generally the speaker need only have a relatively larger information supply than the listener. Even when the knowledge of a listener is vastly superior to that of the speaker, the latter may still speak meaningfully to him. Seldom has an expert in any field considered *all* the ramifications of his area of competence. In the case of the high-energy physicists, though I may not be able to give them new technical information I may yet talk about the moral, religious, or social consequences of their work. At least, I might be able to plead for a way for my field to better understand theirs.

Generally, if a speaker has too little information in an area he can soon acquire enough to handle himself in the speaking situation. There are some subjects, however, that I could not talk about because my audience would not accept my authority. It would be considered presumptuous of me to tell a carpenter how to use a rip saw, but I could tell him the kind of structure I want him to build for me. It might tell the electrician where to put the light switch but not how to install it. By the same token, it would not be appropriate for a student to tell the instructor of a course how the course should be taught, but perfectly appropriate to describe student reaction to the course. In all these cases the question is one of ethos: Can the speaker talk with authority on the subject? Will the listener accept the speaker? Several studies have been made in the area of ethos. In one study the same speech was delivered to two randomly selected groups by the same speaker. In one group the speaker was introduced as a juvenile court judge, in the other he was introduced as a former juvenile delinquent. The speaker contended that the juvenile offender should be treated more leniently. In the case where the listeners thought the speaker was a judge there was a tendency to accept his idea. In the other situation there was significantly more rejection of his idea. In short, the speaker must be able to measure his own ethos in reference to the subject he intends to deal with. He may then decide that all he needs is a bit more evidence, a bit more logical support than a person with somewhat more ethos.

A third factor making a speech on a particular subject impossible is too much information. In most situations time is limited. In five or ten minutes most students would be able to criticize the system of grading used in a particular class. No teacher of that same class could do it in such a short time. He probably could not even begin to define the problem of grading in ten minutes.

3. *What is the listener capable of hearing?*

At a convocation of the University of Denver, the famous astronomer Fred Hoyle lectured on his steady-state theory of cosmology. It was a lucid, nonmathematical treatment of an extremely difficult subject and it was plainly difficult for Professor Hoyle to put his theory in language simple enough for even the sophisticated faculty to understand. Most of the faculty, however, was highly impressed. The students, generally, were bored stiff. They reacted against his raspy voice, his hesitant delivery, and his dull reading. For most of the students and a segment of the faculty Professor Hoyle could just as profitably have spoken in Sanskrit. All that this group could listen to was the external elements of his delivery, for the content had no meaning for them. The audience was incapable of gathering meaning from his language, because they lacked enough knowledge to understand the speech.

The listener may be incapable of hearing a speech for psychological reasons. An extremely conservative person cannot profitably listen to an extremely liberal speaker. An atheist would likely be incapable of listening to a conservative Baptist. When the speaker takes a position and the listener is committed passionately to a polar extreme of that position, there is likely to be little communication. The information coming in to the listener is too violently opposed to what he believes. It is dissonant information. He cannot tolerate such dissonance, so he mentally turns the speaker off and literally does not hear what the speaker says, distorts what he says, or takes such a violent dislike to the speaker that he rejects everything the speaker says.

What happens when the speaker and listener believe in such totally opposite positions that there is no common ground between them? Such an extreme situation is unlikely. Two human beings, no matter how far apart on some things, always have something in common even if it is simply that they both breathe the same air. But the speaker must realize that there are some ideas he cannot reasonably expect certain audiences to hear and much less to act upon. St. Paul recognized this. When addressing himself to the Greeks in Athens he did not simply attack their paganism. He said rather: "I perceive that you Greeks are very religious because as I was walking through your city I saw, among all the other altars to your many gods, an altar marked 'to the Unknown God.' It is this God that I want to talk with you about." When he started talking about the Resurrection most of the Greeks turned him off, but at least he realized that they could not be expected to reject their paganism upon hearing his first sentence. Was his approach hypocritical? Of course not. He merely recognized the adage: You don't shoot your whole wad when you first catch sight of the enemy. At any particular moment in your speech you do not ask your audience to give a response that you cannot reasonably expect from them.

In brief summary, though the source for the intended change is the speaker's main idea, that idea must be selected in terms of a specific analysis of the situation, of the listener, and of himself. The procedure in selecting the main idea may be expressed in the following five steps:

1. The speaker must analyze his own position and express the idea he intends to communicate.
2. He must analyze the position of the listener on the idea he intends to communicate.
3. He must determine the difference between the idea he intends to communicate and the position of the listener.
4. He must determine how far he may reasonably expect the listener to change in the direction of agreement.
5. He must then formulate the specific change he wants his listener to make.

An Example

For a long time I have been discussing *what* you are supposed to do. Suppose I see now if I can show you *how* to do it.

Let us suppose that you are a member of a college class in speech. For some reason your class, probably by the instigation of your instructor, has asked me to speak. The subject has been broadly set as "Education," and being a generous group you have allowed me fifteen minutes, probably because you know that I could not talk for less. Education itself, whatever that is, is too broad a topic for fifteen minutes. Clearly I have to limit it. One way might be to talk about a particular level of education:

Education
    A. Preschool education
    B. Primary education
    C. Secondary education
    D. Undergraduate higher education
    E. Graduate higher education
    F. Postgraduate higher education

What I am listing here are levels which pertain not to education in general, but rather to formal institutional education. Perhaps a prior classification might have been:

Education
    A. Formal
        1. Institutional
        2. Noninstitutional
    B. Informal

Another difficulty is that the first outline above is rather sloppy. Any time you have more than five coordinate points in an outline you can be pretty sure that you have used the wrong unit for dividing the items under the main heading. A better outline might be:

Formal Institutional Education
    A. Lower (twelfth grade and below) education
        1. Preschool
        2. Primary
        3. Secondary
    B. Higher (freshman college and above) education
        1. Undergraduate higher education
        2. Graduate higher education
        3. Postgraduate higher education

The process I have just gone through is simply an attempt to lay out for myself the broad topic within which I must operate. Being an educator in a formal institutional structure I would tend to select that more specific area, and my main interest would fall into the area of higher education.

Since you, my listener, are probably most interested in that which directly concerns you and since the likelihood is that you are enrolled in an undergraduate course, I should probably choose undergraduate higher education as my chief concern for this speech. But this is still an extremely broad subject. How, then, do we get to something more manageable in the time limit of fifteen minutes?

A division of the subject into some arbitrary unit is possible. For instance, we might divide it geographically into United States and foreign and then into Eastern, Southern, Midwestern, Rocky Mountain, Southwest, and Pacific. We might divide it into private and public. We might divide it by cost. These divisions would be valuable to me only if they caught my interest, but my interests do not lie in that direction. A division by function could be made: administration, teaching, learning. These functions correspond to the administration, faculty, and student body. This division is only partly useful for me. I lean toward the belief that the major problems in education are not isolated in any one of the functioning parts of the educational complex, but lie rather in the relations between them. All right, then, what are the problems that occur in the relations between these functioning elements of the institution of higher education?

The Problems Occurring in the Relationships Between Administration, Faculty, and Students
   A. Administration-faculty problems
      1. Tenure, salary, rank
      2. Control of outside faculty activity
      3. Control of the teaching function
   B. Administration-student problems
      1. Student discipline and due process
      2. Financial relationships
      3. Standards and records
   C. Faculty-student problems
      1. Teaching-learning relationship
      2. Social relationships
      3. Grading and evaluation

Since I am a member of the faculty, the problems that arise from the administration-faculty relationship would interest me greatly. They would hardly concern a group of students, unless, of course, I talked about how the problems on this level affect the problems on the faculty-student level. If this were the area that I selected, it probably would be more appropriately considered as a faculty-student problem. Since I am not directly involved in the administration-student relationship, except as it affects my relationship either with the administration or the student, then (B) would not be selected.

My relationships with students have always been rather pleasant. Both my classroom and my social contact with students seem quite easy and relaxed. At all times when those relationships have not been relaxed or pleasant, the problem of grading and evaluation has been involved. I think we teachers say too often that grades really do not matter. We tend to think that the best students do not worry about grades. Such an attitude is extremely naive. When the nature of his job and the salary he commands depends upon his grade rank in college, when he will fail to enter graduate school if he has less than a B average and likely will not be accepted at the school of his choice without a B+ or A, when financial assistance to continue college depends entirely on his grades, how ridiculous to say that he is not concerned or even that he should not be concerned. He would be a fool not to be concerned. Clearly this is the sorest point of contact between the student and the teacher.

Well, we have rather fallen into a subject. Broadly and rather sloppily stated, the subject of my talk to your undergraduate class in speech will be "the problems arising from grading and evaluation in the relationship between teacher and student in undergraduate higher education." What have we then? We have set a rough boundary and said that anything outside that boundary is off limits and we have said that something within it might give rise to a speech.

O.K., what about grades? We can start by asking broad questions and gradually refine the area of concern. Grades: do you like giving grades? No, I hate it. It is the most unpleasant thing about teaching. But that is just a feeling; you can't base a rational judgment on that sort of thing. Why do you hate giving grades? Well, for one thing, it spoils my relationships with many of my students. I would like to think that what I teach has some value for the individual as a human being. I want him to learn the things I know for what it will do for him later. My goal is then fairly long-range, but the student has to be concerned with the grade he will get at the end of the course so he is forced to have an extremely short-range goal. Even ideally the grade is a club to "induce" the student to learn. But teachers are human beings with human biases and the best grades have to be given to those students who conform to the teacher's bias. So, again, while ideally I may wish the student to learn for his own growth and enrichment, the grade forces him to conform to my personal whims and biases.

But does the grade not serve some beneficial function? It has been around long enough; someone must have seen some good in it. I suppose there are those who work harder in a course because they fear a bad grade, so in some sense, it acts as a reward for "good" work and punishment for "bad" work. I suppose, too, that a school has some need for deciding who has lived up to its requirements for a degree. Companies and graduate schools need some standard for making decisions between applicants. Students need some measurement by which they can gauge their progress or the degree to which they have "learned" something or can compare their own achievement to that of others. Teachers, too, ought to have some way of judging how one class compares with another so that he can judge his own performance at various times.

I must admit that at this juncture my own feelings push me toward the conclusion that grades, at least as they exist now, should be eliminated. Generally, I should imagine, students dislike grades as much as I, but most see no ready alternative to them. Nor generally do they like the ambiguity of the situation that exists when the grade is eliminated. Grades, though restrictive, often abusive, and mostly unpleasant, give the student a certain degree of security. It is a system that they have learned to live with and it has become a difficult habit to break.

Most students, then, would probably say that such a plan sounds great but is totally impractical. Some would admit that they are not at all sure that they would work as hard as they should if the threat of grades were removed. An honest few might admit that they could not easily tolerate the freedom of being without grades.

The easiest possible goal for me to reach would be a theoretical acceptance of the desirability of eliminating grades. If I could show the class that it works in some selected instances it would be possible to have them support a wider trial. Perhaps many would say they would try such a course but when it came to getting them to sign up, almost surely most would back out with the excuse that there are too many grade-giving courses that they "must" take. Almost none would dare to throw themselves entirely into such a system.

We are now ready to go beyond the mere mental manipulation of ideas and should be ready to put something concrete down on paper. We are ready, in short, to formulate the specific change through which I might expect you, my listener, to move. Let us interrupt this example for a while and see what must be done.

FORMULATING THE CHANGE

Why is it necessary to put anything down on paper? If a speaker thinks his subject out carefully in his head, isn't that enough? For some it is. However, do not fall into the trap of thinking that the procedure followed in the foregoing example could in any sense be described as adequate. Even if not a single word goes down on paper, the speaker will have to do more than what we have done so far.

Some experienced speakers can work out an idea in their heads and need no further preparation. Most of us are not so facile. Certainly I am not. Working out the idea on paper is perhaps the best way to force yourself into the painful process of ruthlessly evaluating your ideas. Somehow when expressed in cold words on white paper, ideas can be analyzed more objectively than the same ideas in your head. The very act of making sense on paper destroys many ideas at the very start. What seemed good in your head often looks like nonsense on paper.

When finally formulated, the specific change you intended ought to be in the form of a clear, forceful, and complete declarative sentence. Not a question, nor an imperative, nor an exclamation, but a declarative sentence. We will discuss why it can only be declarative in a moment.

Apart from the discipline involved in writing out your idea in a declarative sentence, there are three other goals which the process helps achieve: (1) Working out the idea on paper forces clarity and precision in determining both goals and methods. (2) Paper work sets the mood and tone of the speech. (3) It simplifies the process of organizing.

How do these goals result from merely writing an outline? If a speaker puts his chaotic ideas into a well written declarative sentence, he forces himself to determine the precise relationships between himself and his listener, the listener's ideas and the speaker's own ideas. The speaker must determine fully the action and the actor involved in the proposed change.

Second, it is only when the nature of the intended change is known precisely that a speaker can decide what his goals are, can evaluate their worth, and can choose methods for reaching those goals.

Third, once a speaker has written this complete declarative sentence, his general pattern of organization follows automatically and logically. Generally the basic outline follows in a matter of seconds.

Clearly, if the speaker merely sloppily scribbles the idea onto paper he gains nothing. His goals can be reached only if certain things are true of both the content and the form. Let us consider the content and the form separately.

Content

1. The declarative sentence ought to embody a desired change in the attitude, opinion, viewpoint, behavior, or activity of the listener. Suppose this were my intended change:

Low grades are an unpleasant experience.

This would tell the listener nothing new. Listeners do not grant you their time to hear what they already know. This is not to say that you cannot speak about the unpleasantness of grades. It simply means that if this is the full scope of your subject then, since the listener already has a first-hand experience of this unpleasantness, all you can do that would be of value to him would be to give him a new viewpoint that would perhaps make grades less unpleasant or would deepen and sharpen the experience of receiving them.

We have said already that most students feel that grades, particularly low ones, are unpleasant but that they serve a necessary and useful purpose. An intended change that might be a real change is the following:

> *The giving of grades in liberal arts courses is an unpleasant experience that serves no useful purpose.*

The need for this rule of content is more clearly seen when we are dealing with changes in behavior. On the assumption that the speech of our example is to be given before a speech class, it would be meaningless to use the following as the intended change:

> *The members of this class should enroll in a speech class.*

Clearly the listener has already done what the speaker asks him to do. There is no real change involved. You do not ask people to do what they are already doing or to believe what they already believe.

Another way to state this rule is that the speaker should oppose the *presumption* and therefore accept the *burden of proof.* These are legal terms for the principle we have been talking about. Presumption may be defined as the assumption that what exists at the present is right and good, and what is believed now is what should be believed. It might better be called the tendency toward psychological inertia which makes people hesitate to change their attitudes, beliefs, or habitual patterns of behavior. The result of this inertia is that anyone who wishes to change attitudes, beliefs, or behaviors must create in the listener an imbalance of forces enabling him to make a change. The speaker must upset the balance and dispel the inertia of the listener. Thus the speaker has a burden not simply to assert the change he intends, but to prove that the change should be made.

If the speaker feels he has no burden of proof to support, no presumption to overcome, then there is no point in talking about a particular intended change. He should either forget about talking or attempt a different goal. Even the comedian recognizes this principle. He may be able to get people to laugh at the same joke for a long time, but unless the listener sees something different in the joke, he will not laugh. The comedian who milks a gag-line through a whole routine or even a whole career is able to do it only because each time he uses it, he does it within a new context that makes it newly funny.

2. The declarative sentence must contain the one main idea of the speech. For this reason we may call the sentence *the central idea.* The declarative sentence may be complex but never compound. For instance:

Because the teacher cannot avoid favoring those ideas which conform to his own way of thinking, those courses which deal with the manipulation and interpretation of ideas should not be graded.

This is a sentence with one main and one subordinate clause. It is acceptable as a central idea sentence because the one clause acts in support of the other. The following sentence is not an acceptable central idea:

Grades in a liberal arts curriculum tend to interfere with the goals of such a curriculum and are usually based solely on the biases of the teacher.

As the central idea is constructed, the speaker would be forced to give two different speeches. Unless the speaker violated his central idea almost to the point of rejecting it, the listener could make no connection between the two halves of the speaker's idea. The listener, unable to find a connection, would be confused by this lack of unity and would probably lose both points.

The central idea above might be improved by thinking out the relation between the separate points and spelling that relation out. Thus:

Since it is the goal of most liberal arts courses to encourage the student to deal with, test, and evaluate ideas of his own, any grade which tends to reward the student for merely conforming to the thinking of the instructor would be destructive to the ends of this kind of course.

This would be an acceptable central idea that incorporates both the points of the previous central idea but subordinates one to the other, making the whole a unified concept.

3. The central idea must state or imply the precise response, the exact change, that the speaker wishes to achieve in the listener. It would be a good bet that most unsuccessful speeches are the result of not spelling out precisely the response the speaker expects from his audience.

The administration of this college should eliminate or radically change the 'grading procedures used in the liberal arts program.

Sounds great, but what does it really say? What does the speaker really expect from his audience? As it stands, all the speaker asks is an abstract belief in the desirability of eliminating or instituting a radical but unspecified change in a grading procedure. Now if that is all the speaker intended, fine! But the likelihood is that the speaker intended the passage in the faculty senate of a specific proposal. His intent was to gain active support for the proposal and cause the members of the senate to vote yes on the measure. Put directly, the central idea would be:

This assembly should vote yes on the proposal before it.

The speaker must decide whether he wants the listener to change merely an abstract belief pattern, a peripheral opinion, an attitude, or some behavior. Does he want the listener to be amused, to feel revulsion, to write his Congressman, to riot in the streets? Whatever change he intends should be stated or clearly implied in his central idea. If the speaker cannot include the change in the central idea clearly, how can he expect his audience to be able to respond to it? If he cannot make the response he expects clear to himself, how will he know if the listener does make the intended change?

4. The central idea must imply the mood in which the audience is to respond. This rule is not greatly different from the previous rule. This rule, however, emphasizes the emotional quality of the response the speaker wants from the audience. In rare cases this rule might even supersede the rule that the central idea should be a declarative sentence. Let me illustrate:

Suppose you are debating in the student senate the question of grades. The central idea might be stated:

> This senate goes on record as supporting the elimination of grades in all humanities courses of the liberal arts college.

Clearly the response you want is a yes vote on the resolution. The emotional quality of the response to this proposal would probably be rather clear and cool with little emotional fervor.

The same central idea would probably be inappropriate in a student body rally on the question. Here the central idea might be:

> The faculty is inconsistent and hypocritical when it asks us to deal with ideas intelligently but gives us grades that reflect their own petty biases.

Let us take one further, and we hope improbable, step. Suppose the senate has passed the resolution, the student body has rallied, petitioned, pleaded, been sullen, and uncooperative. It has exhausted all normal channels of disapprobation and petition. It would be nonsense confounded to use either the first or the second central idea. You are now ready to use the ultimate appeal, as Locke puts it, "to the judgement of God and the right of Revolution." What else but:

> To the Barricades!

Only in extreme cases of disorder and disunion is the imperative acceptable. Use it sparingly. There is nothing more disheartening to a speaker than to cry "Havoc" and loose the dogs of war, and have the audience respond: "What are you, some kind of a nut?"

5. The central idea must be so stated that the listener, if asked, could reasonably be expected to respond by repeating the very words

of the central idea. In the debate in the student senate the senators should reasonably be able to respond by repeating the resolution. You'd expect the rally to respond by shouting, "Yes, they are inconsistent and hypocritical for doing that!" And if you could briefly stop the individual rioter, you would hope he would say, "To the barricades!"

The point here is that if you as a speaker could achieve the repetition of the exact wording of the central idea when and if you asked the question: "Can you describe your intended behavior or your opinion, attitude, or belief on this subject?" then clearly you have put together a perfect central idea.

Form

1. Your central idea must be a declarative sentence as opposed to interrogative, imperative, or exclamatory. By now the reason for this rule should be clear. The declarative is a transfer of information. The interrogative merely indicates to the listener that the speaker lacks information. The exclamatory sentence indicates some information transfer but usually only about emotions. Now, clearly, none of the three foregoing generalizations is entirely true. There are some questions that give a great deal of information. It is often important to have information about feelings. Let us try a few and test the consequences of using them as central ideas.

What is the relationship between grades and learning?

At first glance this would seem a good central idea. It points out an important area of concern. But it does not really add anything new to the listener. It does not call for a change. But suppose your object was to cause your listener to question the connection between grades and learning. Then would it not be better to use the following for your central idea?:

The assumption that grades reflect a student's level of learning ought seriously to be questioned.

If you asked the listener for his response you would probably not be satisfied if he gave you back the question, but you ought to be reasonably well satisfied if he responded with the second central idea.

Eliminate grades!

The imperative above may indeed express your ideas. But it implies that the listener is on the point of action and all he needs is the assertion of a command to act. It also implies full power to act. These situations are seldom true when we speak, and therefore to expect the listener to respond to them is both naive and a little foolish. In most cases the more appropriate central idea would be that which advocates the action that will bring about the result intended.

The members of the student body should boycott all elective classes that give grades.

The action advocated may be impractical or even foolish, but the listener is more likely to respond favorably to this central idea than to the first.

An exclamation is simply an outburst of feeling. To bring about any change in a listener it would have to be coupled to a declarative or imperative statement.

2. The central idea must be a complete sentence with a clearly delineated subject and predicate. Churchill said that the English sentence is a magnificent thing. It is, because to construct a good one, the interrelationships between the subject and predicate, between the actor and the action, must be carefully thought out. If these relationships are not thought out the result is often a sentence fragment.

Watch out for the sentence fragment. This kind of sentence has all the external features of a sentence. The words, however, do not express a relationship; they hide one. An example:

Most teachers are dissatisfied in regard to the system of grading related to teaching.

The words "in regard to" and "related to" and others like "concerning," "in case of," "in view of the circumstance that," and "with a view to" hide relationships that the speaker has not thought out. If you ask such a speaker what he means, the chances are that he will not know. Better to say:

Most teachers, though they love teaching, hate to give grades.

3. The central idea should be direct, not indirect. The following central idea is an indirect statement:

I believe that grades tend to discourage the natural curiosity of the student.

What response does this central idea imply? What change does the speaker intend to cause in the listener? Well, if we go according to what is written here, then we must infer that he wants the listener to give up believing that the speaker does not believe that grades tend to discourage curiosity and now believe that the speaker believes it. Sound complicated? Well, that's the trouble. The central idea has added an unnecessary complication. All the speaker really wants to do is to create a belief in the listener that grades do indeed discourage curiosity. The words "I believe that" are pure waste that have nothing to do with the idea and merely complicate the thought. The same is true of the following:

I wish to convince you to enroll in this speech class.

The facts indicate that there is no correlation between grades and learning.

It is generally believed that a student's ability to study independently is related to his ability to get A's.

Unless you want to speak to the points that "you really wish to convince me," or "the facts really do indicate," or that "it is indeed generally believed," in the above cases, then you ought to use the following central ideas instead:

You should enroll in this speech class.

There is no correlation between grades and learning.

A student's ability to study independently is indicated by his ability to get A's.

4. The central idea ought to be active, not passive. This is not a rigid rule. At times a passive mood is justified. The sentence that heads this section is itself passive. The reason it is used here is that if all these rules were put in the active voice they would sound extremely pushy and arrogant. I intended to make them sound more like the voice of reason than outright command. But generally the central idea ought to be active in mood. It tends to avoid an attitude of weakness.

Grades should be eliminated.

You will note that no agent is identified. The listener has no idea of who is supposed to do this. Nor is the method of elimination indicated.

To restate the rule: Unless the context clearly implies a specific actor and a specific action, make the central idea active.

5. The central idea ought to be positive. Again this is not an absolute rule. There are some instances where the intent of the speech is unavoidably negative, as, for instance, when the speaker advocates that a bill be repealed. The psychological effect of negativism is the culprit. A child is sitting quietly coloring in the play room. Mother is about to leave the room so as a precautionary measure she says, "Trumbly, please don't color on the walls." Well, up to that point Trumbly had never associated walls with crayons. Suddenly Trumbly's mother had created a whole new world of fun for him. The point is that to negate something implies that the thing negated is a possibility and one worthy of consideration.

6. As much as possible the wording of the central idea ought to be specific and concrete rather than abstract and general.

The undemocratic nature of student discipline is decidedly unjust.

As it stands, that central idea means almost nothing. Democracy is a highly abstract term. One person's conception of its meaning is likely to differ from anyone else's. When we consider democracy we might picture to ourselves some concrete representation of democracy like the jury box or the voting booth. But these concrete representations of democracy will vary as much as people do. For some, democracy means the right to vote for one candidate.

"Student discipline" is a general word. It involves all sorts of specific elements. There is discipline to suppress or punish cheating, hitting professors, committing a felony, or cutting classes. There is discipline by censure, by manipulation of grades, by suspension, by cancelling late hours, or by expulsion. Which does the speaker mean?

> Expulsion of a student for cheating without benefit of counsel, or without an open hearing, or without the right to cross-examine both accuser and witnesses is unjust according to the due process clause of the Fourteenth Amendment of the Constitution.

It may seem strange to relate the Bill of Rights to student discipline but according to a lower court decision a student in a state college has all of the rights guaranteed to him in the Constitution and he must be treated according to due process. Clearly this last central idea can be argued and argued well.

A SUMMARY CONCLUSION

Please note: Nowhere have I said that if you obey these rules, you'll give a good speech. These are not guarantees, they are advice. Following these rules guarantees only that before you open your mouth you will have molded the idea into a form that at least you can understand. Obeying the rules does not guarantee that your audience has the comprehension that you assumed they did in your preliminary analysis. It does not guarantee that lightning will not strike the building you speak in and disrupt your speech. It does not guarantee that you won't trip and fall. It does force you to think out your idea in terms of its content, your own abilities, and the nature of your listener. I contend that this procedure will increase your chance of doing well.

When the central idea has been thought out, formulated and reformulated, written and rewritten until the speaker is totally satisfied with it, and when he is sure that it conforms to the rules discussed in this chapter, the speaker is ready to draft his preliminary outline. None of the time spent in making sure of the central idea is wasted. The more carefully drawn the central idea, the simpler and more automatic will be the basic outline of the speech. The reason that the next step in the process is so simple is that the basic outline is drafted by a straight-forward analysis of the central idea.

EXERCISES

1. Select a subject area that interests you. Describe five different listeners and indicate for each what central idea you would use. Why?
2. On the general subject "the use of grades in speech classes," develop five central ideas. Indicate what sorts of listeners might respond well to each. Indicate what sorts of listeners would not respond to each.
3. Reformulate the ten central ideas above in terms of the tests for a good central idea for your own class.

READINGS

On selecting subjects, see:

> McBurney, James H., and Ernest J. Wrage, *The Art of Good Speech* (Englewood Cliffs, N. J.: Prentice-Hall, 1955), pp. 79-133.

On stating the intended change in the form of a central idea, see:

> Mills, Glen E., *Reason in Controversy* (Boston: Allyn and Bacon, Inc., 1964), pp. 37-51.

Chapter 3

THE FUNDAMENTAL ORGANIZATIONAL PATTERNS

Let us suppose that by a process such as that described earlier we have analyzed the needs, interests, and ability of the listener and ourselves. According to this analysis, we have arrived at a tentative subject. We have determined what was needed according to the situation. Then by a process of writing, rewriting, and carefully applying the standards of the last chapter we have finally formulated what we think is a good central idea. Our next step is to derive from this central idea a basic pattern of organization.

This fundamental organizational pattern will be a logical one. By logical we do not mean "merely argumentative." We mean rather the quality of being reasonable, being rationally satisfying. It will be logical in the sense that it will be determined by an answer to the question, "What are the logical steps required by the rational listener before he will make the change desired by the speaker?"

There are several reasons for this approach. If we are right in assuming that all formal speaking situations presuppose an intent to change, and since any change in a listener logically requires the overcoming of some sort of mental inertia on the part of the listener that we have called "presumption," then it must follow that any message that we might compose must bear some sort of burden of proof. If this is granted then there must always be a logical core to any speech.

It might well be argued that not all speeches are logical. Some are aimed solely at entertaining or evoking some emotional response. Some may merely attempt to communicate information and therefore have very little logical content. Such a situation, however, does demand logical treatment; first, because no information is without interpretation, and second, no source of information wants that information rejected as valueless.

It must be admitted, however, that some speaking situations are less demanding of logic than others; the situation that exists when a listener expects to be entertained is an example. In this situation it is probable that the speaker would not feel the need to be strictly logical in putting together his message. But at the same time, if he works out that message logically, he will have considered the whole range of possible aspects that he can talk about and thereby can more intelligently choose what to omit or what to emphasize.

Even when there is little logic demanded by a situation, the speaker ought to prepare in the way suggested here: first developing his message fully, logically, and methodically, and then emphasizing those aspects which are most appropriate to the situation.

TWO FORMS OF CENTRAL IDEA

The central idea will be in the nature of a logical judgment. It will take one of two possible forms: simple or complex.

The Simple Judgment

The simple judgment states a relationship between events or objects in reality. It asserts that an object, event, or category A is related in a specific way to object, event, or category B. The following are examples:

Discrete letter grades (A, B, C, D, and F) which place infinitely varied students into rigid, arbitrary categories are unfair.

Grades tend to force students to imitate the thinking of the instructor.

Most students feel insecure when placed in a learning situation where grades are not used.

Failure in many academic courses may be the result of the inability to conform rather than the dullness of the student.

In the first of the examples above the two objects which are related are two categories. The first category consists of those letter grades which are discrete and which place varied students in rigid categories. The second category is that group of things which may be called unfair. In this case the relationship is one of inclusion, that is, the first category is included within the second category. The relationship may be diagrammed:

The second example above indicates a causal relationship between grades and the act of imitating the thinking of a teacher. If put in the form of a strict logical proposition, the central idea would be expressed as follows: Grades (are those things which) tend to force students to imitate the thinking of the instructor. If put like this, the idea can be diagrammed again as a relationship of inclusion, that is, the first category (grades) may be included within the second category (those things which tend to force students to imitate the thinking of the instructor):

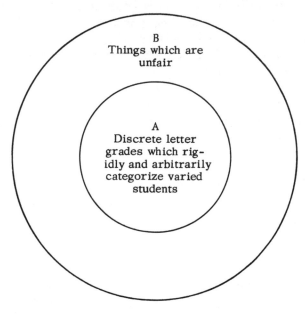

Figure 4

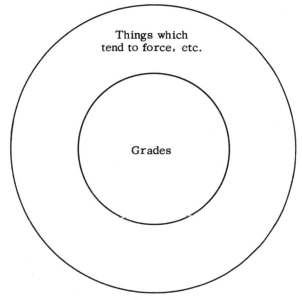

Figure 5

For our purposes here, however, it is enough to say that grades are causally related to imitation.

The third example relates students who are placed in a situation with the feeling of insecurity. The fourth is really a double relation. On the one hand "failure in many academic courses" is related causally to an "inability to conform." On the other hand a causal relation between "failure" and "dullness" is denied. The second relationship here is clearly subordinate to the first and should not be considered a second coordinate central idea.

Being simple judgments, these central ideas claim that a relationship exists. The relationship may be subjective or objective. Most judgments tend to have some subjective element in them. All are based at least in part on our own subjective view of reality. What we generally mean by subjective is that the idea we are stating as a central idea is based substantially on our own value system, and not so much on observable, external data. Clearly a subjective or value judgment and an objective factual judgment are handled in different ways. We will deal with the differences later. At the moment we are concerned with the fact that any simple judgment, whether subjective or objective, is handled in precisely the same way in formulating the fundamental organizational pattern.

Now, since the simple judgment does claim the existence of a relationship, the fundamental organizational pattern must present to the listener the information logically necessary before he can believe the assertion or claim. This information is the reason for believing the claim.

In any simple judgment, two things are necessary for the acceptance of the claim. Some data, facts, or evidence upon which the claim is based is required. The second requirement is a principle, a generally accepted rule, which warrants the mental leap from the data to the claim. This relationship may be diagrammed in the following manner:

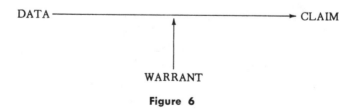

Figure 6

The horizontal arrow indicates the mental leap one must make when he moves from accepting a particular datum to the act of asserting a claim. The vertical arrow indicates the logical support necessary to make the leap. This support comes in the form of a general principle that warrants or allows such a mental leap. Let us take the first example above and see how this would work.

Our claim would be: Discrete letter grades (A, B, C, D, and F) which place infinitely varied students into rigid, arbitrary categories are unfair. In deciding on the two necessary steps of the fundamental organizational pattern, bear in mind what we said before: the basic outline is drafted by a straightforward analysis of the central idea. Simply looking at the central idea should tell you what has to be proved. The data in this case would be: Discrete letter grades place infinitely varied students into rigid arbitrary categories. If this is the data, the warrant should be equally simple to find. What is the only idea that could justify moving from this data to the claim of our central idea? It would have to be the general principle: any system of evaluation which treats varied students in a rigid, arbitrary way is unfair. The fundamental organization of this message then could be diagrammed as follows:

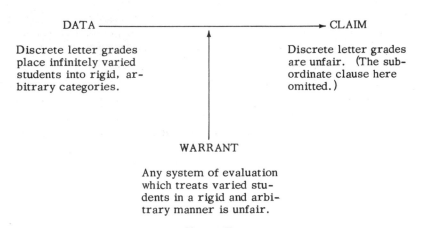

DATA ⟶ CLAIM

Discrete letter grades place infinitely varied students into rigid, arbitrary categories.

Discrete letter grades are unfair. (The subordinate clause here omitted.)

WARRANT

Any system of evaluation which treats varied students in a rigid and arbitrary manner is unfair.

Figure 7

In outline form, the data and warrant would be points I and II, respectively, of the outline.

This analysis should carry you even farther. The data in the organization above is itself a simple judgment and may be treated in the same manner as your original claim. Thus the following argument would result:

The warrant too may be further analyzed. Since it is a general principle, it is somewhat more difficult to argue but something like the following would probably result:

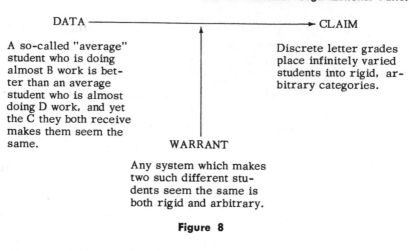

DATA ——————————————————————→ CLAIM

A so-called "average" student who is doing almost B work is better than an average student who is almost doing D work, and yet the C they both receive makes them seem the same.

Discrete letter grades place infinitely varied students into rigid, arbitrary categories.

WARRANT

Any system which makes two such different students seem the same is both rigid and arbitrary.

Figure 8

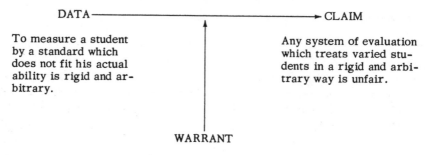

DATA——————————————————————→ CLAIM

To measure a student by a standard which does not fit his actual ability is rigid and arbitrary.

Any system of evaluation which treats varied students in a rigid and arbitrary way is unfair.

WARRANT

A standard which does not fit the actual abilities to be measured is unfair.

Figure 9

This analysis results in the structure of the fundamental organizational pattern which may be outlined as follows:

Central idea: Discrete letter grades (A, B, C, D, F) which place infinitely varied students into rigid and arbitrary categories are unfair.
    I. Discrete letter grades place infinitely varied students into rigid and arbitrary categories.
        A. This system does not take into consideration real and significant differences between students.
            1. Example: A so-called average student who is doing almost B work is much superior to an average student who

is doing almost D work and yet the C they both receive makes them seem the same.
  B. Any system which makes two such different students seem the same is both rigid and arbitrary.
    1. It is rigid because the system cannot adapt to individual differences between students.
    2. It is arbitrary because it is imposed from outside without regard to the real differences present in the student.

II. Any system of evaluation which treats varied students in a rigid and arbitrary way may be considered unfair.
  A. A rigid, arbitrary system is one which does not fit the student's actual ability but rather forces the student into its mold.
  B. A standard that does not fit the actual abilities to be measured is unfair.

Here you have all the necessary steps that must be accomplished if you expect a rational listener to accept this central idea. Clearly you have here a rather stiff and formal outline. It is also incomplete. It would certainly not be your final outline. But notice what it accomplishes. You know first of all that certain things have to be proved. In point IA there is one example. Is a single example enough to indicate that an accepted system does not take real differences between students into account? Could the listener not say that there is certainly a significant difference between the almost-B student and the solid-B student? This is pretty weak data on which to base a whole case. Clearly this speaker would have to do a great deal more than offer one example. The whole of point II is aimed at equating rigid, arbitrary systems with unfair systems. This is a matter of definition. What kind of data is needed for a listener to accept this equation? Is a quote from a dictionary which says "unfair" means "applying a standard which does not fit the thing measured" enough to prove this crucial point? To the speaker it may be enough; to most listeners it is pitifully inadequate. Would analogies of situations where ill-fitting standards were used and resulted in unfair treatment of those measured be adequate for most listeners? Perhaps, if the situations were clearly parallel to the problem of discrete grades and if the results were patently unfair. Even here, you are dealing with a difficult point. The question of whether a system is unfair or not is determined by my personal values—but determined only for my satisfaction. Agreement in such an area is hard to achieve. Perhaps the only way to reach agreement is on specific situations where similar systems have had harsh results on people. If most people looking at the results tended to say, "these people were unfairly treated," then you might reach agreement on the judgment that the system was unfair. Again the question might arise, "was the unfairness in the system or in the way it was applied?"

The outline, then, lets you know where you need support for your ideas. It tells you what sort of support you need. It gives you a basis for judging whether you can really support the central idea adequately. It may even lead you to desert the idea as unsupportable. It certainly lets you anticipate objections.

For instance, the last objection raised was significant for this idea. Does unfairness arise in the rigidity of the grading system or the rigidity of the people who apply it? Is it not likely that no matter how rigid or arbitrary the system might be, if the people who administer it are competent, understanding, and highly human, you would have a totally fair system. If you accepted this argument you would in effect have placed a reservation on your own argument. Let's look at it diagrammatically:

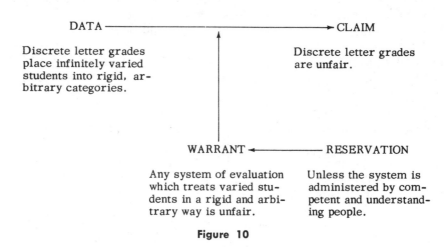

Figure 10

A reservation would tend to qualify or prohibit the assertion of the claim. Anticipating this kind of reservation might lead the speaker to insert a third point that deals with such an objection in advance. In the support of this particular central idea, such a point might be handled in the following way:

III. Though it may be argued that no system is so rigid and arbitrary that good human administrators might not soften it and make it fair, the argument still holds because:

    A. The student could no longer depend upon the formal system that does not vary, but rather on the whim of the man grading.

    B. A person grading by whim is arbitrary and so you have an arbitrary system wielded by an arbitrary man.

       1. This may not be harmful as long as the man is beneficient,

       2. But nothing is to prevent this arbitrary man from making the system even more unfair than it already is.

This argument approaches the philosophical argument that ours is "a government of laws, not of men." The important point here is that such an argument could not have been anticipated without having worked out the idea in some fashion as we have done here.

Facts and Values

At this point we may begin to make the distinction between a value judgment and a factual judgment. We have noted that there are two essential elements in the support of a central idea that takes the form of a simple judgment. These two parts are the data and the warrant. The data is factual observation which, though it may be based on a great deal of further argument, is nevertheless supportable by fairly straightforward, objective, empirical techniques. The warrant, on the other hand, is a general principle which permits the mental leap from the observed data to the claim. The warrant is often a generalization of values. If the data of an argument is the primary question in dispute for a particular listener, then that central idea, for that listener at least, is a question of fact. If the warrant of an argument is the primary question in dispute for that listener, then the question is one of value. In the question of fact, we support the claim by checking the validity and adequacy of our observational technique. In the question of value we check the universality, general applicability, and social acceptability of the values expressed in the backing for our warrant.

The central idea for which we have derived a tentative basic outline could not really be called either a question of fact or value, or rather, it should be considered both. In this case both the data and the warrant are open to serious question, and a listener could reject it either on factual objective grounds or on subjective grounds of values.

Summary

The process of analyzing a simple judgment in itself is quite simple and no one should have much difficulty with it. Perhaps another way of looking at it might make it simpler yet. The central idea that takes the form of a simple judgment is a reaction to the environment. The central idea itself is the statement of the reaction. It may be viewed as the claim of an argument. The data is the answer to the question, "What are you reacting to?" The warrant is the answer to the question, "Why are you reacting the way you are?"

You have probably noticed that in the analysis of the case used for an example at least, neither the data nor the warrant was self-sufficient. They each resulted in a subordinate datum and warrant. How far back do you have to carry this process? Only so far as your listener demands. If your listener will accept your original warrant or data on its face value, you need go no farther. If he will not accept it, you must go beyond it to something he will accept. Remember what you accept as proof is seldom sufficient for most listeners.

What we have done with the first central idea of our four examples should be sufficient to give you a grasp of the principles. If you wish, you might work out the outlines of the remaining three. We will return to the analysis of the simple judgment in our discussion of the complex judgment.

The Second Form of the Central Idea: The Complex Judgment

When the central idea takes the form of the simple judgment, it asks the listener to recognize the existence of a relationship in reality. The recognition of something that was not recognized before is certainly a change. The complex judgment aims at a further change. It aims at creating in the listener an intent to take overt action or to make a conscious mental change. To put it in terms of the medieval faculty psychology which divides the functions of the mind into distinct faculties, the complex judgment attempts to reach the will of the listener; the simple judgment merely attempts to reach the understanding. This statement, as I said, is in terms of faculty psychology. As such it is oversimplified. To try to explain it in more precise terms would take far more space and effort than can be expended here. Let us simply say that the distinction between the aims of the two forms of central idea is that the complex judgment seeks to create an intent on the part of the listener to make an overt change.

In practice there should be no difficulty in recognizing and dealing with the complex judgment. The complex judgment asserts that the hearer "should" or "ought to" adopt a specific policy. If properly worded, the words "should" or "ought to" will appear in the central idea. It asks that the listener or some institution with which he is associated make a change; it asks that something be *done*. The following are examples:

This university should abolish the use of grades in all humanities or liberal arts courses.

This Student Senate goes on record ("should go on record" understood here) as opposing the use of grades at this university.

Speech courses should not use grades.

You may well ask, "What's so complex about these?" They seem a good deal simpler than some of the so-called simple judgments. Their complexity does not arise from their length or the difficulty of their sentence structure; rather it comes from the fact that they ask the listener to go farther than does the simple judgment. Since the listener must move farther than in response to a simple judgment, the normal listener should require more in the way of support before he acts. The complexity of the complex judgment, then, comes from the way in which it must be handled.

The complex judgment requires the assertion and defense of four subsidiary simple judgments for its acceptance. This requirement should be made clear by an example in a medical framework.

Suppose I visit my doctor for an examination. I have been having severe abdominal pain. After a thorough examination, the doctor asks me to sit down and he proceeds to give the following advice:

"I think you ought to go to the hospital immediately and have some surgery."

"What kind of surgery?"

"A gastrectomy; you must have your stomach removed."

"Now, just a minute! What do I have that is so bad I need to have a gastrectomy? Can't you just give me some medicine and get rid of this indigestion?"

"It isn't indigestion you have, it's stomach cancer."

"Stomach cancer! I'm finished then—what good will surgery do?"

"Cancer, even cancer of the stomach, is not incurable. I think we found it early enough. There is a good chance we can get it all. But we've got to operate right away. Every day we wait your chances of surviving go down."

"What are my chances right now?"

"Well, about fifty-fifty. But they're the best you'll ever have, and without surgery you don't have any."

"Isn't there some other way to get at this thing? Chemotherapy, maybe, or X-ray?"

"I know the thought of surgery is not very pleasant, but a gastrectomy is your best chance. We might get to it with some of the newer chemotherapy but so far it hasn't proved too effective. You'd probably have about a 10 per cent chance of getting through it."

"But I only have a 50 per cent chance with surgery!"

"Well, that's a lot better than 10 per cent, and if we can get it before it spreads your chances are even better."

"Look, I'm not a rich man. How much is this going to cost?"

"Well, if everything goes well, it will cost you several thousand dollars over the next few years."

"What about the other costs—I mean the ones you don't count in dollars?"

"The operation is a painful one. If it's successful, you'll have to change your style of living considerably—be careful about what you eat, the exercise you get."

"So what I'm doing is weighing my chances for living against those costs. If I lose, then the costs are transferred to my family. It's not an easy choice."

"No it isn't, but you have all the information I can give you to make it. You know what you have and how serious it is. You know how likely a cure is. You know how effective the remedy is. And you know what it will cost you whether you make it or not. I'm sorry to be so blunt with you, but you're the one who has to choose."

He's right. Under that circumstance he would have given me all the information I need. I am not at all sure how I should choose in such a situation. The illustration may seem a bit macabre, but it brings out clearly the four subsidiary simple judgments that must be supported when your central idea takes the form of a complex judgment. You will have noticed the issues the doctor dealt with:

The first was the nature of the disease. Before anyone will make a change from the *status quo,* the way things are now, he must be shown what is wrong with that *status quo.* In the case of the doctor, he indicated that his patient had cancer, which could be fatal. For convenience, let us call this the *ill.* This issue will include two parts: a statement of the condition and an evaluation of its seriousness.

The second issue the doctor dealt with was the question of the curability of the disease. If the patient was going to die no matter what was done, if the disease or ill is truly incurable, there is no point in continuing the conversation and there is no remedy. The second issue then that any listener will demand is the issue of *curability.* Is the difficulty, the ill that creates a need to change the *status quo,* something that can be changed?

The third issue is the remedy. Will the remedy really alleviate the ill, will it solve the need? If the remedy will not really get rid of the illness, the central idea should be rejected. Call this the *remedy* issue.

Finally the doctor dealt with the cost. Is that financial, physical, moral, or spiritual cost that one has to pay too high for the remedy? I suppose one way of solving the trauma of getting grades is to drop out of school. Indeed, some people have paid that cost to eliminate the ill, but was it really worth it? Ultimately does not the dropout suffer more from the remedy than he does from the ill? If any remedy costs too much it deserves to be rejected. The last issue, then, is that of *cost*.

To summarize, any complex judgment may be analyzed by the following four issues:

Ill:	I. There is a serious problem which needs a remedy.
	A. The problem is of a particular nature.
	B. The problem is serious enough to require a remedy.
Curability:	II. The problem is curable.
Remedy:	III. This particular remedy will be effective in curing the ill.
Cost:	IV. The cure will be worth the cost.

We should note that in treating any particular central idea it is not always necessary to use all of these issues. These issues constitute a complete support of a central idea but it may not always be necessary to be complete. Some listeners might be fully aware of the problem, and so *ill* might be eliminated. Often there is no need to deal with the curability of an ill. In some instances the remedy might be so obvious to everyone that the only task the speaker has is to get people to act. Often the cost is so insignificant or the listener so fully able to afford it that it need not be mentioned. Complete support of a central idea of this type should use all four. Note, too, that if the listener demands that a speaker deal with an issue, the speaker must deal with it. If the listener is dissatisfied with the speaker's treatment of any one of these issues, logically he must reject the central idea. If someone wished to argue against the central idea, he would logically have to refute only one of these issues. Depending on the requirements of the listener, the speaker would emphasize, de-emphasize, or even omit one or more of these issues.

When the speaker asserts any one of these issues he is making a simple judgment. This means that in working out the fundamental organization the speaker derives a great deal from that central idea. He derives his four major points. For each, he derives at least two subordinate points. And in the *ill* issue he will derive even the third level of subordination.

An Example

The most efficient way of demonstrating how this method of organization works in practice is to apply it. We will take one of the sample central ideas from the beginning of this section on the complex judgment.

Let's use the short central idea, "Speech courses should not use grades." This central idea is not perfect by any means. It is negative and somewhat indirect. If we assume that the message is to be delivered to that same speech class that was the listener in the last chapter, then the message might better be directed toward the abolishment of grades in this particular class. Being reasonable, however, I would realize that few speech classes have that option. I am therefore dealing with a theoretical proposition: in effect my listener is asked to believe that grades should be abolished. Let us take this central idea, then, as being equivalent to asking the listener to believe that "This speech class should abolish grades." Implied here is the conditional clause, "if it could." The basic outline, bearing in mind our previous analysis of the listener, would be something like the following:

Central idea: Speech courses should not use grades.
    I. The use of grades in a speech course tends to violate the purpose of such a course.
        A. Since the purpose of a speech course is to develop the ability in a student to think independently and to cultivate his own individual style of speaking, grades, because they impose the thinking and style of the instructor on the student, violate the very purpose of the course.
            1. The purpose of a speech course is to cultivate independent thinking and individual style.
                a. Every speech teacher since Aristotle has praised these two qualities in a speaker.
                b. A speech course should aim to cultivate that which speech teachers praise.
            2. Grades tend to impose the thinking and the style of the teacher on the student.
                a. The teacher must reward with the grade what he thinks is best and punish what he thinks is worst in the speaking of his students.
                b. Being human, he must think highly of the thinking and style that most resembles his own.
        B. If the grades really do violate the purposes of such a course then this is a problem that should be solved.

    II. The reasons for using the grade in a speech course are not fundamental to the purpose and intent of the course and therefore could be removed without damage to the course.

    A. Grades are used merely as a form of academic bookkeeping for the administration of the institution and not for any educational value they might have.

    B. The removal of grades, therefore, though it might force the administration to revise its methods of record-keeping, would have no effect at all on the effectiveness of the course in reaching its goals.

III. The removal of the grade would free the student to think on his own and strive to develop his own individual style.

    A. The removal of the grade would prevent the teacher from exercising *punitive* restraints upon what the student says and how he says it.

    B. Since the student would no longer fear the consequences of being an individual, he would feel freer to develop himself.

    C. Though it might be argued that this would also remove the opportunity for the teacher to correct the bad habits or techniques of the student, this would not be true since the teacher could still criticize and argue.

IV. Such a measure would tend to increase the mutual respect of the student-teacher relationship without putting an undue burden of responsibility on the student.

    A. If the teacher wished to correct the student, he would have to convince the student of the rightness of his position without resort to the "force" embodied in the grade. The respect for the teacher's judgment, then, would be based solely on his greater experience and the force of his rationality.

    B. The student would, indeed, be on his own and though this prospect is rather frightening for the student who has come to depend on the safety of grades, once he gets used to the freer relationships that exist without grades he develops faster and with greater depth of knowledge.

This outline would constitute the speaker's basic organizational pattern. You will note a few things about it. First, it grows out of a straightforward analysis of the central idea on the basis of the four issues: *ill*, *curability*, *remedy*, and *cost*. It may be that upon further analysis of the speaker himself, of the needs and requirements of the listener, and the nature of the situation in which it is to be given, some of the parts of that pattern may be eliminated or expanded. There may be a great deal of rearrangement.

Second, it is made up of complete sentences and spells out in some detail the lines of argument that the speaker intends to follow. The reason for writing out the lines of argument in some detail is that only in this way can the speaker discover his errors before it is too late. One of the worst catastrophes for any speaker is to be pounding at an argument before a listener, only to discover that it cannot be defended. It also makes clear to the speaker where his support must be placed, the nature of the support needed, and how much. For instance, in point IA2a, the bland assertion that the teacher *must* reward and punish in a particular way is probably unprovable. After consideration the speaker may decide that a better argument would be that most teachers tend to reward and punish in this way. His data to support this claim perhaps would be a list of examples of teachers that do it, an expert opinion that it is generally done, or an argument about the human tendency to praise the thinking that is most like our own. The three warrants that would be used to relate these three pieces of data to the claim would be (respectively) (1) These examples are a sufficient sample to justify the generalization of the claim; (2) This expert is qualified to make the generalization expressed in the claim; and (3) Since this is a universal characteristic of almost everyone, teachers are subject to it.

You will notice, too, that A and B under point IV include a great deal of material that could probably be expanded into a more careful outline. Each of these subordinate points contains within it the fragments of data and warrant and in one case reservation and backing. Upon further consideration the speaker might expand these fragments into full-blown argumentative structures: perhaps as follows:

IV. Such a measure would tend to increase the mutual respect of the student-teacher relationship without putting an undue burden of responsibility on the student.
   A. The measure would tend to increase the mutual respect of the student-teacher relationship.
      1. The teacher would base his correction and evaluation on the force of his experience and the rationality of his opinion.
         a. The teacher must either command respect from the student by the force of his rationality and experience or by the use of the grade.
         b. To remove the grade as a weapon would force the teacher to depend upon rationality and experience.

  2. A relationship based on rationality commands more respect than one based upon the coercion of a grade.

B. The measure would not put an undue burden of responsibility upon the student.

  1. Though for some students the increased responsibility of governing their own behavior in the learning process without the coercion of grades is at first frightening and often somewhat painful,

  2. If the discomfort results in the achievement of something better, it is not an "undue" discomfort.

   a. Once students become used to freer relationships, they develop faster and do better in their studies.

    (1) (Examples here of students who performed better because of the freer atmosphere.)

    (2) (The warrant that this sample is enough to generalize to most students.)

   b. To develop faster and to do better in one's studies is a goal that makes the discomfort worth it.

Here again by spelling out the lines of argument we are able to detect potential weaknesses: for instance, the assumption that a teacher has available only two means of commanding respect, contained in point IVA1a. This is clearly a false dilemma. The speaker would want either to change the argument or support it and he had better not wait until a sharp listener catches him on the horns of his own dilemma—that smarts too much.

SUMMARY

What is the point of all this? From a straightforward analysis of an adequately stated central idea we can derive the fundamental logical structure for our message. We can analyze beforehand all of the potential strengths and weaknesses of our ideas. We can anticipate where we need support or correction. And we know precisely what kind of support and how much we need to flesh out the message.

The result is a fundamental pattern of the logically necessary elements of the central idea sentence. In no sense is this outline to be dogmatically followed in every situation. It should be rigorously followed only where rigorous logical proof is demanded by the listener, and even in that situation the particular arrangement of points and the way in which they are presented must be adapted to the intelligence, bias, and mood of the listener.

This pattern should provide a reliable guide to further research. The speaker should know precisely what too look for to develop an adequate message from this basic skeleton. He can adapt it to the needs of the situation by the judicious selection and careful use of particular kinds of material and various forms of subsidiary organizational patterns.

EXERCISES

1. Formulate three simple central ideas and three complex central ideas on the same subject; for example, "grading procedures in this class."
2. Develop the issues of one simple and one complex central idea from the six above.
3. In the six central ideas of Exercise #1, indicate where the presumption and the burden of proof lie.
4. Fully develop four arguments in support of the central idea: The use of grades in a speech course thwarts the goals of that course.
5. Fully develop four arguments against the same central idea.

READINGS

On the fundamental patterns of organization see:

HULTZEN, LEE S., "Status in Deliberative Analysis," in *The Rhetorical Idiom*, D. C. Bryant, ed. (Ithaca, New York: Cornell University Press, 1958), pp. 97-123.

TERRIS, WALTER F., "The Classification of the Argumentative Proposition," in *Quarterly Journal of Speech*, XLIX (October 1963), 266-273.

On Toulmin's structural logic see:

TOULMIN, STFPHEN, *The Uses of Argument* (Cambridge: Cambridge University Press, 1954).

Chapter 4

RESEARCH:
THE MATERIAL

We have now reached the real work stage of putting a message together. The speaker must now go out and get the material he needs if his listener is to accept his idea—not just any material, but the most effective he can find. The nature of the material will be determined by the nature and emotional content of the idea, the nature and mood of the listener, and the nature of his own personality. The rule of selection we may call the rule of "best evidence."

TWO TYPES OF MATERIAL

Material used in a message may be looked at as evidence or as illustration. These two types of material are similar in that they seek the same end: assent on the part of the listener to the central idea. They differ primarily in the way in which they are presented and the mood in which they are heard. Let's look at each type in turn, starting with evidence.

Material as Evidence

We tend to call the material supporting the central idea or the subsidiary ideas evidence when it supports those ideas in a logical way. When we use evidence we hope the listener will infer from it the idea we are supporting. When we say that evidence is good or bad we tend to mean that the evidence does or does not lead directly and logically to the idea we support. I use the word "tend" because being logical is not at all that simple. One man's logic is another man's nonsense.

Evidence may be classified in three ways: experimental, observational, and testimonial. These are listed here in the order of best evidence, that is, experimental evidence, whenever available, is the logically best evidence.

Before we deal with the individual types of evidence, let us take a more extensive look at evidence in general. Evidence may be viewed simply as that material the speaker feels that the listener will accept as fact. If the listener will not accept it on its face, the speaker must offer further argument and evidence until the listener is satisfied. What constitutes evidence, then, does not depend on the speaker at all, but rather on the listener. The speaker may be fully convinced by the merest scrap of fact—for him this is evidence. But since the speaker wishes to change the listener and not himself, his criteria for evidence are worthless unless they agree with the criteria of the listener.

You will remember that we said that any claim asserts a relationship existing in reality. Evidence, then, is a statement acceptable as true to a listener from which, by means of the proper warrant, he may infer the claim of the argument.

Does all this mean that we simply manipulate our evidence to please the listener? This sounds decidedly unethical. This, however, is not a statement of what the speaker should do. It is a warning that no matter what he does, the final judge of whether the listener will accept evidence is the listener himself. Does this mean that there are no objective rules of evidence? No, but it does mean that whatever rule of evidence you use, you cannot expect it to be universally acceptable to everyone. It may come to the point where the only evidence a listener will accept seems illogical to you. At that point you must make a choice. If using illogical evidence is the only way to change the listener, do you use it?

It is almost certain that if Socrates had said, "Yes, I have corrupted the youth of Athens and I'm sorry. As punishment I will go into voluntary exile for a year," he would likely have enjoyed a delightful vacation in the islands and returned to teach again. Instead he chose to deny the charge. He insisted that he was not only righteous but was the salt that preserved Athens and that he be rewarded rather than punished. Athens killed him. The question arises, would we remember him now if he had chosen otherwise?

Well then, can we suit our evidence to the intelligence of the listener? It is indeed possible for you to sneak weak evidence past a stupid listener; but to rely on his stupidity is dangerous. It is far safer to select and handle your evidence by the highest standards you have and run the risk of offering too much. We shall deal with those standards as we look more closely at the various types of evidence.

Experimental Evidence

Experimental evidence is objectively the best form of evidence. That is, if we accept the Western concept of the scientific method as valid, this is the best form of evidence. The reason for the qualification is that though most of us like to think of ourselves as scientific, few of us really act that way. Witness the almost indisputable evidence that smoking is a direct cause of lung cancer and the millions of unbelieving or, at least, unresponsive smokers in this country. We tend to believe that which supports our present *modus vivendi* and doubt that which contradicts it.

Experimental evidence results from a carefully controlled situation in which an independent variable is manipulated while the change in a dependent variable is observed. Under experimental conditions all the elements of the condition which might affect the dependent variable are held constant, while the single element whose relationship to the dependent variable you wish to discover is either allowed to vary or is caused to vary. If this is not clear, the following example should at least make it less obscure.

Suppose you wish to discover the influence of a grade upon the learning of a student. This is not an easy relationship to discover. Let us see if we can construct an experimental situation that would measure this relationship. It seems reasonable to argue that if we could put two similar groups of people through precisely the same academic course, the one group being graded, the other ungraded, any difference in learning would be due to the presence or absence of a grade. Basically the argument is sound. Difficulties arise, however, when we try to eliminate any other variable that might also have an effect upon learning. Let us take the problems of two similar groups. We might take a single group and divide it into two at random. The theory of random distribution would assure us that given a sufficiently large number of people divided into two groups at random, any variable that might affect the outcome of the experiment would be divided equally between the groups. There are statistical rules for determining the chances for an unequal distribution based on the number in the sample.

Another method would be to use matched groups. This would be accomplished by matching members of one group with the members of another on the basis of any variable the experimenter believes might affect the dependent variable, in this case the student's learning. And so members of the two groups might be matched in height and weight, sex, age, educational background, socio-economic level, nationality, and as many other factors that the experimenter believes might be relevant. The two methods might even be combined.

The next problem is the measurement of the dependent variable. First the experimenter must define the variable. Does he mean merely the retention of factual material? A carefully worked out objective test might be used. Does he mean a set of skills? A panel of experts might be asked to judge the students by means of a standard set of criteria. Does he mean by learning a change in attitude toward something? An attitude test of some sort might be used. In any one of the three methods the validity and reliability of the measuring instrument would have to be checked. By "validity" is meant the assurance that the instrument actually measures what the experimenter says it does. By "reliability" is meant the consistency of results using the same instrument over time; that is, if a thermometer measured the temperature of an object differently in two instances when actually the temperature of the object remained constant, then the thermometer can be said to be unreliable.

Finally, to be sure that the results of an experiment are trustworthy, the experimental situation must be held constant in both groups with the single exception of the independent variable—in this case the presence or absence of a grade. Ideally, for instance, the teacher in both groups should be identical in all significant respects, an obviously impossible requirement. Perhaps the safest method would be to have two teachers who met the different groups at the same time of day but swapping classes at random. The nature of the room in which the classes were taught would have to be as close to identical in all significant respects as possible. The nature of the material presented, the way in which it was presented, the nature and quality of the teacher's advice and criticism, the personality of the teachers, and the interpersonal relations between teacher and students would all have to be carefully controlled. The testing procedures would have to be the same. In short, everything but the presence or absence of a grade would have to be the same in both groups. Ideally even the pattern of irrelevant, unrelated events occurring in the two groups would have to be controlled.

Even after the experiment had been run under rigorous standards, the problems of statistical treatment and accurate report would remain. Any difference at all in the measurements of the two groups is not an adequate evidence of the relationship between grades and learning. The difference has to be statistically significant, that is, the experimenter has to be reasonably certain that the differences he observes are actually attributable to the manipulation of the independent variable and not simply to some chance variation. Again we return to the theories of random variation. When any characteristic is measured in any normal population, there will be a mean measurement around which most of that population cluster. But there will be a minority of that population that deviates somewhat from that mean and a few that deviate greatly. As one moves farther and farther from the mean the chances of encountering another member of that population decrease rapidly. Thus, the probability that the differences measured by the experimenter occur merely by chance must be calculated, and the degree of certainty acceptable in this calculation varies with the nature of the things measured and the importance of the result. For instance, if a machine part costs five cents to replace and the consequences of its failure are insignificant, we will tolerate a rather low chance that the part will survive over a period of time. If, on the other hand, the part is expensive or if the life of the user depends upon its proper functioning, we will tolerate little less than certainty that the part will last. The same is true of an experimental result. Often the arbitrary figure of .05 degree of uncertainty is selected as a cut-off point. This means that we will accept odds of five chances in one hundred that the results are due to chance and not to the independent variable. In other situations we demand .005 or no more than five chances in a thousand that the result is due to chance. The more critical the result the more certainty we demand.

The reporting of the experimental result is subject also to close scrutiny. Ultimately the experimenter can claim that the relationship he asserts is valid only for his experiment and only to the extent justified by his measurements. In the experiment described above, he could claim only that the presence or absence of a grade produced the difference measured by his instruments. Whether this constitutes a difference in learning depends on the validity of the instruments and whether the thing measured really was learning and not simply factual recall, the ability to perform a skill, or a particular change in attitude.

The reason for the foregoing lengthy analysis of experimental method was to show that though experimental evidence is the best possible, it is also the hardest to come by. One other factor ought to be borne in mind when you discover a piece of experimental evidence. Make sure that you are not talking about cause or effect when the evidence merely shows correlation. If the experimenter is reputable he will be very careful about his claims. Only in rare cases does a reputable experimenter claim to have discovered a cause. This is especially true in the social sciences. An experimenter will usually say only that there is a certain degree of correlation between an independent variable and a dependent variable. What he means is that the two are related in some way, but he cannot be certain that the relationship is one of cause and effect.

Observational Evidence

The next best evidence is observational. Another name for observational evidence is "empirical." The word "empirical" is usually reserved for that type of observational data that is gathered through careful scientific observation. "Observational" is a broader category that includes both scientific and unscientific data.

In observational evidence the individual who observes may simply report, describe, or "tell about" an event or a series of events, or he may attempt to measure variables in the event he is watching. The observer may attempt to measure attitudes on a subject or a shift of opinion on an issue. He may record real estate prices over a ten-year period or sample the Graduate Record Examination scores over a ten-year period of students graduating from ten midwestern colleges. He may simply describe an accident he witnessed on the corner near his office or report his observations of the total eclipse that he watched from a hillside. He may describe the behavior of a rat in a maze or record the mating behavior of gorillas in the Kenya jungle. All of these may be used as observational evidence in an argument.

We may make two major distinctions in observational evidence on the basis of what is reported:

Examples

Examples are single events. The observer notes, records, and reports the occurrence of a relationship in his environment. It may be direct evidence of that relationship. If the point in question is whether A killed B and I saw the event occur or someone else saw the event occur, this is observational evidence that A did indeed kill B. It may be evidence that an event can occur. If the point in question is whether an iceberg collision can do sufficient structural damage to sink a modern ship, the citation of the example of the *Titanic* would indicate that such a relationship or event is possible. An example may also support a generalization. If I maintained that grades discourage independent initiative on the part of students, then a single example in which it could be shown that grades were the cause of such a discouragement would support the generalization that all grades tend to discourage such initiative. Note that I said "would support" and not "prove." Proof for such a generalization would have to include a sufficient sample of all situations where grades are used and some reasonable assurance that no instance where grades did not discourage initiative would turn up. A single negative instance would disprove the generalization.

A sum of examples may also be used. Often the term "figures" are used for such a sum of examples. An observer may report his experiences with ten classes in which no grades were given and give the results numerically. He may report that of the 156 students involved in these classes, 63 per cent showed an increased interest in school. These are simply the sum of many individual examples. Figures, then, are not really distinguishable from examples.

Statistics

An observer, however, may not simply sum up the examples which have come to his attention; he may go beyond mere addition and begin to draw statistical inferences and judgments about the figures. He may wish to determine the central tendency of the examples he has observed. He would then proceed to derive a mean, compute standard deviations, and perhaps place the examples on a curve, plotting one variable in the relationship observed against another. He may compare one variable against another to discover any significant correlations between them. Statistics, then, are large groups of examples to which have been applied certain procedures to determine the significance of the examples.

Our primary concern about such evidence is the validity and accuracy of the observation. An observation may be made under scientifically controlled conditions, by a meticulous scientist looking for precisely defined relationships. Or it may be made by a myopic drunk through the windows of a speeding car on a dark street. Three questions should be asked about observational evidence:

(1) What were the conditions under which the observations were made? That is, were the conditions suitable for accurate observation? The famous story of Lincoln defending a client on a murder charge illustrates the importance of this question. The case hinged on the eye-witness account of one John Cass, who claimed that he saw Lincoln's client commit the crime. The witness claimed that he could make positive identification at night over a distance of fifty yards because of a bright moon. His testimony, however, was thrown out since at the time the observation was said to have been made, the moon had not yet risen. Under the circumstances no one could have been identified at such a distance.

(2) Was the observer capable of making the observation? That is, did the observer possess all the necessary abilities to make the observation? In the motion picture, *Twelve Angry Men,* the piece of evidence holding back the jury from acquitting the defendant was the eye-witness account of a woman who claimed to have seen the defendant stab the victim. Her testimony indicated that while she was lying on a couch she had looked across the street and through the windows of a moving elevated train she had seen the defendant commit the murder. The difficulty of seeing anything through a moving elevated train was estimated as not impossible for adequate observation. One of the jurors, however, had noticed that the witness had two marks on the bridge of her nose indicating that she customarily wore glasses. The jury reasoned that if she had been lying on the couch she would not have been wearing her glasses and

therefore would not have been able to make a positive identification. The defendant was acquitted.

(3) How precisely was the observed relationship being defined? That is, was the relationship that the observer reported actually observable?

> PROSECUTING ATTORNEY: Tell the court, Mr. Edwards, precisely what you observed through the window of your neighbors' apartment.
>
> EDWARDS: I saw that man (Let the record show that Mr. Edwards pointed at the defendant) murder . . .
>
> DEFENSE COUNSEL: Objection! The witness is making conclusions.
>
> JUDGE: Sustained. I direct the witness to confine himself only to what he saw.
>
> PROSECUTING ATTORNEY: Continue, Mr. Edwards.
>
> EDWARDS: Well—he stabbed her.
>
> PROSECUTING ATTORNEY: You mean you saw the knife enter the victim's body?
>
> EDWARDS: Well—not exactly. I saw that man raise his hand over her head, then I saw his hand come down and then this awful scream, and the police found her body and she had been stabbed.

Clearly the defense counsel could rip the observation to shreds. The defendant was the victim's karate instructor and the scream was merely the natural accouterment of the sport. Someone else must have done the deed. At this point the camera pans across the courtroom and zooms in on the sweaty face of the real culprit.

Another question that might be asked in the case of statistical evidence: What were the nature and quality of the statistical manipulations used? In most cases, depending on the reputation of the source, this question need not be asked. Notice, however, that this introduces a new consideration: the reputation of the source.

In very few cases will the speaker who uses the evidence be the same person who collected the evidence. In most situations the speaker discovers the evidence in a report made by the original experimenter or observer or even in some secondary source. Clearly, to the degree that a piece of evidence is not first-hand with the speaker, to that degree the evidence is neither experimental nor observational, but rather testimonial. Therefore, almost all of the evidence a speaker uses is fundamentally testimonial evidence.

Testimonial Evidence

Testimonial evidence is evidence that we get from someone else. The critical point here is our trust in the source giving the evidence. If we do not trust it, we won't accept its evidence. If we do trust it, we accept its evidence. Unfortunately this is true no matter what the merit of the evidence. It is the rare individual who accepts the report of an enemy or denies the report of a friend. In practice what this means is that if there are two equally valid pieces of evidence, one from a source the listener likes, the other from a source he dislikes, the listener will most likely accept evidence from the source he likes. Making a choice of evidence in such a case is quite simple. Decisions are more difficult when the best evidence, logically considered, comes from a source the audience will not accept while an inferior piece of evidence comes from an acceptable source. Whom do you satisfy? Your own logical standards or your listener's prejudice? Satisfy his prejudice and perhaps achieve the intended change; satisfy yourself and fail with a free conscience: the choice is no easy one.

There are two general areas of concern in handling testimonial evidence: the nature of the testimony and the nature of the testifier.

1. *Nature of Testimony*

Testimony may range all the way from the report of a scientific experiment to the ranting of the worst sycophant. Broadly viewed, testimony is any opinion. The opinion may be a reliable statistical inference. It may be an inference based on those statistics or an interpretation of them. It may be a judgment or an evaluation even further removed from the original statistic. It may shade gradually into broad policy judgment and philosophical speculation. At the opposite end from an experimental report, it may be nothing more than a schizophrenic flight of fancy.

If the nature of the testimony is experimental it should be evaluated as the results of any experiment would be; if observational, as any observation would be. If, on the other hand, the testimony is merely the inference, evaluation, or judgment of an individual, it must be judged in cither or both of two ways: on the basis of the trust you place in the man, or the trust you place in his inference-making procedures.

We will deal with the evaluation of the source in the next subsection. The evaluation of the source's inference-making procedures depends on the speaker's ability to reconstruct the argument by which the source reached his conclusion. The questions the speaker would ask himself about his own fundamental pattern of organization should be applied to the evaluation of a source's inferences. Does the warrant justify the leap from the evidence to the claim? Is the data sufficient to make the claim? Are there any serious reservations to the validity of the warrant? Is the claim sufficiently qualified? If the source's procedures come out favorably there is little more the speaker can do except appeal to the source's reputation for trustworthiness. If any of these questions cannot be answered, the validity of the inferences must remain in question.

2. *The Source*

Testimony may be divided into expert and lay testimony. By expert testimony we mean inferences and opinions that a man is qualified to give by education or experience. The examples that come most readily to mind are the expert witnesses used in trial law: the ballistics expert, the chemical analyst, the handwriting expert. Generally the law will allow inferences and judgments only from a man qualified as an expert and will allow only first-hand, direct observations from all witnesses not qualified as expert.

An expert witness, however, is allowed to make inferences only in his own special field of expertise and in no other. Probably former President Eisenhower would qualify as a military expert and perhaps as an expert on the Presidency, but certainly not in economics or nuclear physics.

The law admits the testimony of the layman only on matters that he has himself experienced and will allow him no inferences or judgments.

These two types of sources may be treated in the same way when evaluating the evidence derived from them. In evaluating the source the following questions may be asked:

1. What are the qualifications of the source to give this kind of information?
2. Was the source in a position to know or discover the information?
3. Is the information internally consistent? Does it anywhere contradict itself?
4. Is the information consistent with other facts that we are sure of?
5. From our past experience with this source do we hold it trustworthy?
6. Is the source neutral and unbiased on this subject?

Perhaps a final question would be whether the source is acceptable to my listener. It may be unfortunate but it is nevertheless true that most of any individual's information is accepted on trust. We have learned that we cannot function without a measure of trust in our fellow human beings upon whom we depend for information. From childhood we have trusted our parents to teach us accurately. We tend to believe what our teachers tell us. Seldom do we question the veracity of our newspapers, or the television newscaster. The books we read are generally trustworthy to us. But a mark of maturity is probably the ability to question the sources we usually accept.

Ultimately you must face the fact that as a speaker—no matter how airtight your logic and conclusions are—your listener has the final say about his response. If he does not like the way you comb your hair, the way you wear your clothes, or the accent with which you speak, and he allows himself to be influenced by these, you have no hope of reaching the change you intend for him. It is his right to trust whom he will and he will exercise that right.

It is, in a sense, this problem of trust with which the next section about material as illustration deals.

Material as Illustration

First of all, there is no essential difference between evidenciary and illustrative material. That which determines whether a piece of material is evidenciary or illustrative is the use made of it and the mood in which it is handled. Since it is not materially different from evidence, illustrative material may be classified in precisely the same way as evidence.

Use

Let's deal first with its use. Illustrative material is not used for logical proof but rather to gain the emotional assent of the listener. It is aimed at relating the listener emotionally to the speaker's idea or with some object or idea which in turn is related to the speaker's idea. The object of illustrative material is to cause the listener to identify with those objects, persons, or ideas which relate favorably with the speaker's idea and to disassociate with those objects, persons, or ideas which relate unfavorably with the speaker's idea.

Identification

The concept of identification needs some definition. In the diagram below L represents the listener and I the idea which the speaker wishes the listener to accept, the desired change. O represents any other object, idea, or person.

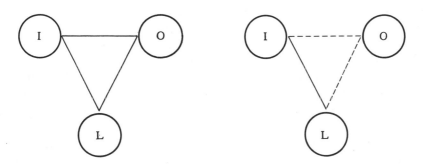

Figure 11

The objective of the speaker is always to create a strong positive identification between L and I. This identification may be described as a love, desire, or admiration for I. Such an identification is represented by a solid line. Disidentification, which can be hatred, disrespect, or rejection, is represented by a dotted line. If the speaker can show that an object, idea, or person with which L already identifies is in turn identified with I, there will be a tendency for L to identify with I. If, on the other hand, the speaker can show that an object with which L fails to identify is in turn disidentified with I, there will be a tendency for L to identify with I. Put in the terms of Aristotle, we tend to love the friends of our friends and the enemies of our enemies.

The question arises, what creates the original identification between O and L? Simply that we identify with those persons, objects, or ideas which seem similar to us, which we perceive as having characteristics like our own, or which we can imagine to be like us. We disidentify with those persons, objects, and ideas which we perceive as different or foreign to us.

Suppose then the speaker faces a listener having had no previous contact with him. With whom will that listener identify and how does the speaker use this principle of identification? The speaker has a choice. He may use an identification that the listener already has and show that the person with whom the listener identifies believes in the speaker's idea. He may seek to create an identification with someone agreeing with his idea. Finally, he may seek to make the listener identify with him.

If the speaker chooses to capitalize on an already existing identification, he will likely choose an authority whom the audience respects or believes and show this authority as approving of the speaker's idea. Many people, for instance, respect the opinion of Hyman Rickover in the area of education. If I can show that Admiral Rickover supports my proposal to eliminate grades, the listener will tend to favor my idea to the degree with which he identifies with Admiral Rickover.

Another form of pre-existing identification that might be used is a more emotional form of argument than the use of a respected authority. I might, for instance, argue that schools that use grades actually harm the child. If I can then show that the listener's children may be harmed by the use of grades, I have associated my idea with one of the strongest identifications. The parent identifies with his child; the object, grades, is shown to threaten the child (that is, is disidentified with the child). The parent, therefore, disidentifies with grades. To carry the thought one step farther, since the parent disidentifies with grades and sees that my proposal disidentifies with grades, the parent will support my proposal.

Creating a new identification is more difficult. One of the best examples of this kind of persuasion is the advertising of the Save the Children Federation. The typical ad shows the picture of a lovable child, describes the sorry condition of the child, and asks the reader to contribute, not to the federation, but to the child through the federation. The reader is expected to identify with the child. Having identified with the child, the reader will wish to help, love, and desire good for the child. If the federation helps the child, the reader will wish to help the federation.

In creating a new identification the speaker must remember that the listener will identify with those persons who are like himself or those close to him. If the child in the advertisement is not like the readers' own children or like the children the reader might have, the reader will have a lower tendency to identify with the child.

Finally, the speaker may ask the listener to identify with the speaker himself. To do so the speaker must present himself as a person who is like the listener, who is like him physically, socially, morally, who likes the same things, does the same things, thinks the same thoughts. To the degree that the speaker so presents himself, to that degree will the listener identify with him. The listener, generally, sees himself as a man of intelligence, good will, and high moral character. These, then, are the characteristics that the speaker must generally evince. It is usually dangerous however simply to claim these characteristics for yourself. They must be demonstrated indirectly through the choices the speaker makes. He must make the choices that the listener would make when acting at his best.

Modes of Presentation

The primary tool in establishing identification or disidentification is the mode in which the presentation is made. There are three modes: exposition, narration, and description. I will describe these three methods here. The point is to show the relevance of these modes to the processes of identification.*

Exposition defines a process, object, or idea. It analyzes its parts and synthesizes it as a whole. For instance, if we were to exposit or "expose" a particular educational system, we would define it as a whole. We would then break it down into its parts and define each part. Perhaps we would talk about the administrative functions, the teaching function, the facilities, the student function. Finally, when we had defined, described, and

---

*If you wish to get more information about their use, consult a source like George G. Williams' *Creative Writing* (New York: Harper and Brothers Publishers, 1954).

explained the parts sufficiently, we would synthesize the whole by show-
ing how the parts of the educational system work together to fulfill the
goals of the system as a whole.

Identification comes through exposition in that we identify with that
which is clear, understandable, and interesting. These are the purposes
of exposition: to make something clear, interesting and understandable.
We disidentify with that which is obscure and frightening. If our object
then is to make the listener disidentify with something, then we must
use exposition to make the process, object, or idea appear obscure and
frightening, or complex, or dull and boring. This is not to say that when
we aim at creating disidentity we use exposition poorly. This would make
the listener disidentify not only with the idea but also us. Our aim here
should be to present as clear, understandable, and interesting a picture
of the bad qualities of the process, object, or idea with which the listener
is to disidentify.

Description is usually far more effective in creating identification. The
reason for this greater effectiveness is that description aims at creating
a vivid mental picture of some object. We tend to identify or disidentify
more easily with what we can see. Pictures are probably far more effective than words. To the degree that a description creates a vivid mental
image, to that degree it will be effective in establishing identity.

Wartime propaganda on both sides illustrates how effective description can be and also illustrates how it is used. Atrocity stories have always
been used. First of all, the atrocity is committed against someone with
whom we do identify and this person is described in such a way as to
resemble us. The atrocity is then described with enough vividness to
make us feel the pain of the victims. We then are expected to hate the
person who commits the atrocity: he is described so as to make him
seem strange, unusual, and evil.

The effectiveness of description arises from the fact that the listener
makes his own identification. The speaker merely presents the verbal
picture in terms that are vivid and concrete. The listener then identifies
with that in the description which is familiar, warm, and comfortable
for him and disidentifies with that which is unfamiliar, cold, or frightening.

In putting a description together, the speaker ought to let the description do the work. The speaker should never have to say: "There,
isn't that warm and familiar." If he does the listener will tend to say,
"No, it isn't." The description should be in terms as specific, concrete,
and vivid as the speaker can use. The description should be straightforward and should avoid the judgments of the speaker as much as
possible. The judgments and evaluations of the speaker should be con-

veyed by the selection of the elements of the description. If disidentity is the aim of a description, the terms should be dark, cold, unfamiliar, and frightening. If identity is the object the terms should be warm, bright, and familiar.

Narration is probably the most effective method of establishing identity or disidentity. Narration presents a character more vividly than he can be presented in any other way. It includes description but extends far beyond it. The character must be placed in a situation and he must be acting toward a meaningful end. You yourself can recognize the power of a story in creating an identity between you and the hero or a disidentity between you and the villain. Can you ever forget Ishmael or Captain Ahab, David Copperfield or Uriah Heep, Othello or Iago?

The modes of presentation, then, are the means of making material illustrative. This does not imply that as material becomes more illustrative, more likely to create identifications, it becomes less evidenciary. On the contrary, the ideal in every speech is to have the maximum of both evidence and illustration. The ideal material in any situation is the best evidence presented in descriptive or narrative form creating the strongest possible identification of the hearer with the ideas of the speaker.

Suiting the Material to the Situation

The speaker should always try to use his material in such a way that it is both the best available evidence and the most effective illustration. Different situations call for different uses of material. The material should be suited to the disposition of the listener. For instance, he may have only slight interest in the speaker and his subject. Under this circumstance the speaker would not attempt to establish strong emotional identification. He would probably simply try to maintain the interest already present or perhaps amuse and entertain the listener. The speaker must realize that if a listener has only shallow interest and wants him to go out and fight in a dangerous cause, the likelihood of immediate change is slight. The speaker may make his plea, but he must do a great deal of arousing before he can make it *effectively*.

In other circumstances, the listener may be actively hostile to the speaker. Another listener may be totally committed to the cause of the speaker. The important point is that the speaker may not ask the listener to do anything that is not justified by the present disposition of the listener.

A speaker may have a strong interest in his subject, but even a strong interest does not justify the speaker in going farther than giving information. The listener may be emotionally stimulated to some degree or he may strongly agree or disagree. This justifies the speaker in engaging in some dispute. Finally the listener may be committed to the point of view of the speaker to some degree. At this point persuasion toward further commitment and overt action is possible.

It is important that the speaker make a careful judgment about the disposition of the listener before he speaks. He must never ask too much of him. The result is usually that the listener will turn against the speaker.

This is not to say that the speaker may never be radical in his demands, that he may never ask much of a listener. On the contrary, the speaker is not worth much who does not ask much of an audience. He must only realize that at any given point in the speech he must not ask too much. He must educate the listener to the point where he will accept the speaker's demand. Even during the speech the speaker may not go beyond what the disposition of the listener justifies.

If the speaker sees the listener relaxing in his chair or actually yawning, that is definitely not the time to ask for money no matter how worthy the cause. A person's disposition toward your ideas may be adequately judged through such external signs as posture and muscle tension. If a listener is leaning forward, is obviously tense, it is safe to assume that he is highly involved in what you are saying. He may be involved negatively, he may hate you, but at least he is involved; you no longer have to worry about getting and maintaining his interest. If he is leaning toward you and nodding yes to every point you make, you have a committed listener and can go a long way with him.

The speaker must be constantly alert for nonverbal signs of interest and attention in the listener. He must judge at every point in the preparation and even in the actual delivery of the speech whether it is reasonable to expect a listener to respond positively to what is being said. If it is not reasonable, don't say it.

A NOTE ON HUMOR

This is a cautionary note. Humor is an effective device; it can also be dangerous for the speaker. Humor is the injection of incongruous elements into what we have called illustrative material. The dangerous aspect of incongruity is that it may also be incongruous with the identification that the speaker wishes to establish. We cannot laugh at someone with whom we have identified. If we have identified with someone and then the speaker makes that someone the butt of a joke, either we must lose the identification or become angry with the speaker. We may laugh *with* those we have identified with. To laugh *at* someone we must be at least partially disidentified with him.

SUMMARY

In dealing with the material which supports your central idea there are two controlling questions, "Where do I stand?" and "How far can I reasonably expect my listener to move toward my position?" If these questions are answered systematically and fully, the speaker can be sure that he has thought out his own position adequately and has sufficiently analyzed the listener.

EXERCISES

1. Classify the material used in a controversial newspaper editorial.
2. In the same editorial, diagram two arguments. Criticize the data and warrant in each. Indicate what forms of evidence appear in the data.
3. Rewrite the arguments as you think they should be and/or indicate what sort of evidence and what sort of warrant would have been better.
4. Take three magazine advertisements and three television commercials and analyze them in terms of the principle of identification.
5. Analyze the argument in one advertisement and one television commercial.

READINGS

On evidence and its use see:

MILLS, GLEN E., *Reason in Controversy* (Boston: Allyn and Bacon, Inc., 1964), pp. 97-123.

On the principle of identification see:

BURKE, KENNETH, *The Rhetoric of Motives* (Cleveland: World Publishing Company, 1962).

Chapter 5

RESEARCH:
THE SOURCES

There are just two sources for the speaker's material: his own first-hand experience, and the written and oral reports of the experiences of others. In this chapter we will deal primarily with the second source, the written and oral reports of the experiences of others. A few words about first-hand experience should suffice.

The value of your own first-hand experience varies according to how carefully you have observed. If you are a scientist and your experience is experimental in nature, your report is likely to be considered reliable if you have followed the rules of good scientific investigation. We talked about those rules in the last chapter. In most cases, unless you are an expert in the field in which you are speaking, your first-hand experience will carry little weight with a listener. Let this be noted, however: first-hand experience, wherever it can be used, is probably the best kind of evidence. It should not be used when your listener will not accept you as an authority. Most of you who read this book will not be authorities to most listeners in most areas.

The second best source for materials is the second-hand report of the investigator made directly to you. If in the course of your speech someone should ask, "How do you know that Dr. James B. Conant believes that?" if you can answer, "Because last week when we were having coffee together he told me so," then clearly you have scored a point with your listener. We should add a caution here: you have scored a point only if your listener will accept your mere word about your close relations with James B. Conant. It must seem reasonable to him that you are likely to be on intimate speaking terms with your source.

INTERVIEWING

Suppose one of your points was that the students feel anxious about grades. How do you back up a point like that? One way would be to say, "Well, grades always made me anxious, and I assume other students feel the same as I do." That is your first-hand experience and as such constitutes a legitimate piece of evidence. The question, of course, is whether you can speak for other students. In this situation the survey method is probably the best technique.

Survey Interviewing

Compiling a survey is not a simple task. You don't simply work out a set of questions and pass them around to your friends. First of all, a survey must be standardized. That is, you must be sure that whenever and wherever it is to be used the same questions mean the same thing to the people questioned. The same questions to two different groups of people may in effect be two different questions. A question phrased in French would be answerable by one group, unanswerable by another. A question given to a college graduate may mean something different to a Puerto Rican in a New York slum. It isn't enough to say that you will explain the question to the slum dweller for then again you are not asking the same question.

The questions in any survey must be phrased so as to mean the same thing to the entire population of which they are to be asked. It must use no words that will have one sense to one group and another sense to another group. Let me illustrate: To most of us the word "snail" calls up the image of a small crustacean that leaves a slimy trail. To a large segment of the Southerners, however, a snail is a sweet roll that one would customarily have with coffee. To most of us a "poke" is something we get if someone is angry with us. To many it is a bag one might carry groceries home in.

In formulating a survey the form of question used is an important issue. Will the answers be quantifiable, that is, will they be in such a form that they can be treated statistically? Consider the following two questions:

The second question is clearly quantifiable. The first question could not only not be quantified, but it is also likely that you would get few similar answers even in outward form. The second question limits the alternatives of the respondant but you can treat the answer statistically. On the other hand, the first question gives the respondant a chance to use his own set of standards and might lead you to a dimension of affect or emotion that you had not considered. For instance, a student might reply that though he read less he read more deeply and understood more of what he read. The second question would give you a negative effect;

the first would give you at least some idea that having no grade helped studying.

What we have said so far is true of that sort of interviewing which aims at surveying the opinions of many people on the same subject. The results are usually tabulated and handled statistically. A more common type of interviewing demands a different approach.

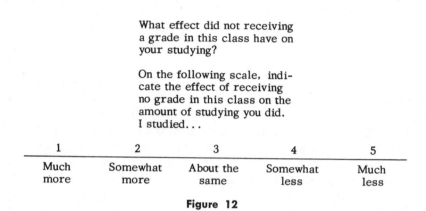

What effect did not receiving
a grade in this class have on
your studying?

On the following scale, indicate the effect of receiving
no grade in this class on the
amount of studying you did.
I studied. . .

1	2	3	4	5
Much more	Somewhat more	About the same	Somewhat less	Much less

Figure 12

Personal Interviewing

Personal interviewing is far more common than survey interviewing. This interview occurs when someone wishes to get the opinions of a single person on a subject. Its aim is not to get a tabulation of opinion, but to get a deep understanding of one man's thinking on a subject. The approach in this situation is precisely the opposite of survey interviewing. The questions asked the interviewee should generally be open-ended so that he can give a full exposition of his opinions on the subject.

The questions used in a personal interview should be carefully planned so as to get at the opinions that you need. Avoid loaded questions that put the interviewee on his guard. Your object should be to put him as much at ease as possible. The object should never be simply to argue with him or make him angry. You want him to make as objective a statement of his opinions as possible.

Taping is the most effective way of recording the responses of the interviewee. These responses can be typed up later. In whatever manner the interview is recorded, accuracy is most important.

We have spent little space on the use of first-hand material and of the second-hand interview because, in almost every case, your main source of material will be the printed page. It is this source that will take up the rest of this chapter.

PRINTED MATERIAL

Let us approach the use of printed material in a practical way. Let us take the speech outline of Chapter 3 and see how we would go about getting material for such a speech. We will take particularly point IV of that speech since it contains the contention that needs most support: that a student develops faster and with greater depth of knowledge when no grades are used.

The first useful tool that should come to mind is the card catalogue of the library. The subject catalogue under Education, Marks and Marking Systems, Educational Evaluation, and the like might yield some books related to your topic. For instance under Education—Experimental Methods, you can find a book by William H. Burton called *The Nature and Direction of Learning*, a recent book which, according to the catalogue card, explores recent trends in teaching procedures. According to the card, the book also contains bibliographies that may give you some leads to even more useful books. Burton's book is fairly recent and so should bring you almost up-to-date on important books in the area. Another book, *Revolution in Teaching* by Alfred DeGrazia, is an evaluation of new theory, technology and curricula in teaching. This book, too, contains bibliographies that may be useful. A third book, by Don H. Parker, is called *Schooling for Individual Excellence*. This book, according to the information on the card, is not likely to be too useful, but since the aim of your speech seems to be similar to the intent of the book's title, it might have some value in defining your own goals for the speech.

After looking at such books as these, you should be ready to go on to the relevant periodical literature available to you. The *Reader's Guide to Periodical Literature* will probably be your first thought. By looking under Education, Grading, Marking Systems, and the like, you can get a fairly good idea of what popular articles have appeared on the subject. To stop here, however, is a common but bad mistake. You want information that will support your contention that a gradeless system is better for the student. The more scientific that information is, the more likely it will be believed. Popular magazines are not likely to contain the best evidence in this field. You need to turn to specialized professional journals.

Many fields have specialized bibliographies and indexes. If you feel that there might be useful information in a specialized source, your best course is to consult a guide to specialized bibliographies. The most convenient and useful one I know is *Guide to the Use of Books and Libraries* by Jean Gates. This book lists specialized areas and discusses the various sources available in that area.

The two most important sources available in the field of education are the *Education Index,* which catalogues periodical literature in educational journals just as *Reader's Guide* does in popular periodicals, and the *Encyclopaedia of Educational Research,* which summarizes research in education.

In the *Education Index* one discovers the following articles:

Grades in Speech. W. H. Bos. *Speech Teacher* 15:86-8 Ja '66.

There should be no F's; students should be judged on the basis of whether or not they are achieving their potential. G. Bloom. *Bsns Ed World* 46:13-14 Mr '66.

College grades and adult accomplishment; a review of research. D. P. Hoyt. *Ed Rec* 47:70-5 Wint '66.

College teaching without grades; are conventional marking practices a deterrent to learning? G. Mannello. *J. of Higher Education* 35:328-34 Je '64.

Clearly these four articles seem relevant to the point you are trying to make. Since the contentions made in all of these articles are similar, if not identical, to your own claim, it is likely that their evidence will be helpful to you. This is especially true of Mannello's article in the *Journal of Higher Education.*

In the *Encyclopaedia of Educational Research* the article on "Marks and the Marking Systems" is pertinent. Though the article reports no research on gradeless systems, it reports considerable research on the practices of grading. Research indicates, for instance, that girls are graded higher than boys, that women teachers grade higher than men teachers, that teachers tend to grade well-liked students higher than their performance justifies, while disliked students are graded lower than their performance justifies, and that students at intermediate levels of acceptance are marked on a chance basis. These findings seem to indicate that grades tend to be unreliable as indicators of student performance.

The foregoing is a brief example of the kind of material that can be found to support the specific claim of the speech we are using for illustration. Remember that the specific research that one does is a secondary concern. The first concern is to establish the structure of what you are going to say. Once you have done this, you don't have to waste time reading sources of questionable relevance. You can go directly to materials which you need. There are four types of reference works that ought to be considered when looking for specialized information:

Indexes

Any index *indicates* where the information you want may be found. As we have said, the most familiar indexes are the card catalogue in the library and the *Reader's Guide to Periodical Literature*. An index is designed so that you can look up a subject heading like "Marks and Marking Systems" and discover what information is available and where it may be found. This is true of the index of a book or any specialized index. The most important types of indexes are periodical and newspaper indexes.

Each index covers a particular kind of periodical. For instance, the *Reader's Guide to Periodical Literature* indexes articles appearing in magazines and journals of general interest. The *International Index* indexes articles appearing in foreign periodicals as well as American journals in the areas of the social sciences, the humanities, philosophy, and the like. The *Education Index* indexes books, periodicals, and pamphlets in the field of education.

Examples of other specialized indexes are: *Business Periodicals Index, Applied Science and Technology Index, The Art Index, Essay and General Literature Index, Book Review Digest,* and the *Catholic Periodical Index*. This is only a small sample of the indexes available to you. The best index to indexes you can find is a helpful reference librarian.

Bibliographies

All of us are familiar with the bibliographies that we find in books. Again, however, there is a far greater diversity to bibliographies than most of us are aware. In preparing for a class about the public address of Sir Winston Churchill an indispensable aid was a special bibliography on Churchilliana. A bibliography is usually a list of books dealing with the same or similar subjects. Most useful bibliographies are annotated to some degree, describing the content and/or significance of the listed books. Fortunately in this area we are aided by an index: *The Bibliographic Index* is a subject index of current bibliographies that appear in book form, in pamphlets, or as parts of books or periodicals.

There is almost no end to the number and kind of bibliographies available. It is almost safe to say that there is a specialized bibliography for any area in which your interests might lie.

Dictionaries

Dictionaries, too, are familiar to us all. A dictionary may be defined as any alphabetical listing of words or names and their meanings, history, usage, significance, classification, and/or pronunciation. Dictionaries may be classified as to their purpose or their subject. There are pronouncing dictionaries, dictionaries of antonyms and synonyms, dictionaries of usage, dictionaries of slang. In the form of research with which we are dealing here, dictionaries classified by subject area are far more important.

For instance, an indispensable aid in any Greek or Roman classical research is the *Oxford Classical Dictionary.* There are a large group of biographical dictionaries like the *Dictionary of American Biography* or the *Dictionary of National Biography,* which lists notable inhabitants of Great Britain or her colonies. *Who's Who* and *Who's Who in America* are other biographical dictionaries. In this area of biographical dictionaries there is again an index that will lead you to the proper source: the *Biography Index.* There are additional dictionaries such as *The Dictionary of Philosophy, A Dictionary of Psychology, Dictionary of Philosophy and Psychology, The Catholic Encyclopaedic Dictionary, Oxford Dictionary of the Christian Church, Dictionary of Social Science, American Business Dictionary, Dictionary of Education, Guide to the Space Age, Dictionary of Modern Ballet, Dictionary of World Literature,* and dozens more.

Most of these dictionaries not only define terms, but present informative articles on significant topics within their special areas, just as an encyclopaedia would. In fact, there is no essential difference between dictionaries and the next category of research aids, encyclopaedias.

Encyclopaedias

According to the Greek derivation of the name, encyclopaedias attempt to give information about the whole circle of the arts and sciences. Encyclopaedias in special areas attempt an exhaustive treatment of topics in that particular field. Most encyclopaedias are alphabetically arranged and are therefore no different from dictionaries except perhaps in scope or depth. In fact, many dictionaries are called encyclopaedias or cyclopaedias and some encyclopaedias are called dictionaries.

Besides well over a dozen general encyclopaedias, there are such specialized encyclopaedias as *The Oxford Companion to Classical Literature, The Reader's Encyclopaedia, Encyclopaedia of Concert Music, Larousse Encyclopaedia of Astronomy, Cyclopedia of Education, Encyclopaedia of American History, Encyclopaedia of the Social Sciences, Encyclopaedia of Religion and Ethics, An Encyclopaedia of Psychology,* and *The Concise Encyclopedia of Western Philosophy and Philosophers.*

Similar to both dictionaries and encyclopaedias are specialized handbooks like those in chemistry, engineering, social psychology, and the like.

These four types of research aids will help you locate the specific information that you need. The next question is, what do you do with the information when you get it?

HANDLING THE SOURCE

The first thing the researcher does with his source is decide whether it is useful and reliable. You must learn to cross-examine that source just as you would if you were interviewing the author. You would not simply accept the results of the author, but you would try to find out his methods of arriving at those results. Then you would judge the value of that information as you would evaluate any piece of evidence.

The primary criterion is whether a piece of material satisfies your needs. Your detailed outline tells you precisely what kind of information you need, and you should always be aiming for the best evidence available.

If you decide that the information contained in a source is indeed valuable, note-taking is the next step.

Note-Taking

Jacques Barzun, in his excellent book with Henry F. Graff, *The Modern Researcher,* says that "a note is first a thought." He is commenting here on the usual way most people take notes. There is a tendency either to quote the source verbatim or, by cutting out the connectives, simply to compress the source to fit the note card. This makes the note difficult to handle when you come to the point of putting your idea together.

Select out of the source not the words but the idea you need, then cast it in your own words in the way you intend to say it when the time comes to deliver it. In this way you insure that the source's idea has been absorbed and digested and it assures that the information will fit into your idea as well.

SUMMARY

The only way you can be sure of doing what has to be done in the most economical manner is to let your detailed outline guide you in all aspects of research. It tells you what information you need. It suggests what kind of evidence you need. The detailed outline tells you what sources and what specific information is relevant and worthwhile. Without the guidance of that detailed outline, the library is chaos and research is equivalent to wandering without compass or map. Time spent in developing your central idea and the detailed outline is never wasted. You win it all back in research.

Exercises

1. Develop three central ideas that you would use for your speech on three widely different topics. Indicate your rationale for each central idea.
2. Indicate in detail what sources are available to you in locating material for each central idea.
3. Develop one of these central ideas and research it thoroughly. Present an annotated bibliography of your research.
4. Present all the material you would use in a speech on a set of 3" x 5" cards.

Readings

On research practices see:

Barzun, Jacques, and Henry F. Graff, *The Modern Researcher* (New York: Harcourt, Brace and Company), 1957.

On using a library see:

Gates, Jean, *Guide to the Use of Books and Libraries* (New York: McGraw-Hill Book Company), 1962.

Chapter 6

THE SUBSIDIARY PATTERNS OF ORGANIZATION

We have said in Chapter 3 that there are two fundamental patterns of organization. When the central idea takes the form of a simple judgment, the fundamental pattern requires data and warrant and may have a reservation. When the central idea is a complex judgment the fundamental pattern would require the four subsidiary simple judgments asserting ill, curability, remedy, and cost. We indicated earlier that these fundamental patterns are not absolute; they can and should be modified to fit the situation.

As examples of modifications that might be made in these patterns we cited situations in which all of the steps might not be necessary. For instance, where the listener already knew the extent of a problem and its seriousness it would be acceptable to leave out the assertion of an ill. We indicated that often the curability issue was unnecessary. In the case of a simple judgment either the data or the warrant might be emphasized even to the exclusion of the other. When the real point at issue was a choice between values and the data was agreed upon, the data might be omitted entirely. When the facts were at issue and the values implied in the warrant were agreed upon or were unimportant, the warrant might be deemphasized or even omitted.

These fundamental patterns are logical organizations in that they follow a logically necessary development. As such they are arbitrary and conventional. Any logical pattern is based on some sort of symbolic system accepted as a convention. Hopefully there is something in the real world that is at least analogous to that conventional system that we accept. The primary reason for our accepting the logical system, however, is that it maintains our intellectual comfort; it satisfies our intellectual need for rigorous standards of procedure. Logic is a pattern we impose upon our symbolic representations of our world so that we may more effectively deal with those symbols. It is subjective in that it satisfies a need in us and only secondarily conforms to some objective structure in reality. Again hopefully, the more universally accepted logical systems also conform to objective reality—they would not have survived for so long unless they not only gave man inner satisfaction but also made him more effective in dealing with the world.

The logical patterns of organization, then, are neither wholly subjective nor wholly objective. We are dealing with a hierarchy of organizational patterns by which we give order and structure to our knowledge. The hierarchy moves from the wholly objective along a continuum to the wholly subjective. Since man's knowledge can only be symbolic in nature and since symbols are created by man, then strictly none of man's knowledge can be wholly objective. Only reality itself is objective. Man's knowledge approaches that objectivity but never reaches it.

At the next level above objective reality stand descriptive systems for organizing our perceptions of reality. We often speak of these patterns as being organizations according to reality. They are based upon our ways of handling space, time, matter, and motion. Among these patterns of organization are (1) the chronological, which organizes events in the temporal order in which they occurred; (2) the purely spatial, in which events are ordered by some consistent pattern of directions in which the events were observed, such as from one side to another, from top to bottom, from closer to us to farther from us; (3) the relative-spatial, in which objects are spatially compared to each other such as when objects are placed in order of size, height, or relative position or motion; and (4) relative-perceptual, in which objects are ordered according to the energy levels of the perceptual stimuli reaching the observer from them, such as organization by brightness, loudness, clarity, or sharpness. These four examples represent what may best be termed descriptive patterns of organization.

At the next level above the purely objective and the descriptive patterns of organization stand the logical patterns of organization. The fundamental patterns of organization that we have discussed form the general structure in which any particular logical pattern may be expressed. Some of these logical patterns, however, may be used as subsidiary patterns in support of the fundamental argumentative structure.

Among these logical patterns of organization there is a whole group based on an analytic-synthetic concept. One example of this type is the pattern based on the part-whole relationship. The analytic pattern would be a statement of some whole, like a machine, and its analysis into its constituent parts. The synthetic pattern would take the parts and describe how the parts fit together to form the whole. Another example is the general-particular relationship. The analytic pattern would derive particulars from a general statement. This would be a deductive pattern. The synthetic pattern would move inductively to derive the generalization from a group of particulars. Similar to the example of the general-particular pattern is the abstract-concrete pattern. In this pattern the analytic phase would be the movement from an abstract concept, like justice, to concrete expressions of the concept like jury systems, laws, law enforcement, and the like. The synthetic phase would be the movement from concrete events to some more abstract concept or symbol which relates them, for instance, the conceptualization of a language system from the observation of concrete written symbols of an undeciphered language.

Another type of logical pattern is that based on cause and effect relationships. In practical terms of outlining, such a pattern would state a cause, and its effects would be listed in subordinate points or an effect would be stated and the subordinate points would list its causes.

Finally, at the opposite extreme of the objective-subjective continuum, are what may best be called the valuational patterns. At the outset it must be said that no pattern of organization is free from the influence of the organizer's values. There are, however, patterns of organization which are purely subjective. Patterns that order points by relative importance, impressiveness, beauty, or utility are based wholly on the values of the observer. When such a pattern is used it tells more about the individual using it than it does about the speaker's subject.

There are, then, three classes of organizational patterns which may be used as subsidiary patterns of organization to further develop or modify the fundamental patterns. The most objective is the class of *descriptive patterns,* the next most objective are the *logical patterns,* and the most subjective are the *valuational patterns.* Let us discuss each of these classes of organizational patterns in terms of (1) the nature of each class of patterns, (2) how they relate to the fundamental patterns, and (3) some specific types of organization that appear in each class.

DESCRIPTIVE PATTERNS

The descriptive patterns of organization constitute the ways we deal with our objective, observable reality. They are based upon the way we observe that reality. To understand what is going on in descriptive organizations we have to make a basic distinction: we must understand the difference between a "presentational" event and a "discursive" event.

As I am sitting at my typewriter, in my office, there are things going on around me. There is an infinity of potential stimuli moving around and toward me. There are the light stimuli coming from the typewriter, paper, and the print on the paper. These are the stimuli to which I am now giving the most attention and which are therefore most clear in my consciousness. There are stimuli that reach me through my peripheral vision, the light and movement that come from the window or through the open door. These I am conscious of, but I am not paying direct attention to them. There are the sounds of the typewriter, of a lawnmower outside, of children playing outside, and of someone walking in the hall. There are the pressures exerted by the chair I am sitting in, of my fingers on the keys, of my feet on the floor, the feelings I have of the temperature of the room and a breeze that riffles the paper on my desk, the smell of freshly cut grass and someone drinking coffee in another office. All of these physical energy transfers impinge all at the same time upon the space I occupy. They "present" themselves in a single, undifferentiated, continuous flow. The whole of this flow of energy is a presentational event.

The event we call a painting is another example of a presentational event. It may indeed be true that the painter used only one brush at a time, applied one color at a time, and put his picture together one element at a time. Nevertheless, when I look at the painting all of the elements, lines, shapes, colors, impinge upon my space at the same time and all togther. There is no objective way of distinguishing between any of the energy transfers moving from the surface of the painting to me. They are presented to me all at once.

But clearly I am incapable of dealing with all of these potential stimuli in the same presentational manner. My observing them and, even more, my thinking of them are entirely different sorts of events. When I look at a painting I will not see it as a whole unless I am far enough away from it to make the details undistinguishable. In observing a painting, the eye will fixate on a particularly prominent feature that falls wholly on the macula of the eye, that portion of the retina where vision is sharpest. This impression is "registered" in the brain, the eye moves to another prominent feature, and a new impression is registered. Apparently when an event is recorded on the brain that event becomes, not a presentation, but a series of electrical impressions connected by movements of the sense organs also recorded as electrical impressions. What was presented all at once now becomes a series recorded bit by bit. The observation of an event, then, is a discursive event.

One step farther—if I should communicate a description of this event to another person, this would necessarily be a discursive event. No matter which method I chose of transmitting a description of the event I had experienced, it would still be discursive. If I chose to paint or draw a representation of the event the lines and colors and shapes would move from my brush or my pencil in a series of connected strokes. If I should try to describe the event musically, one note would follow another. If I should attempt to describe the event in language, one vocal sound would follow another, one word and one gesture would follow another.

In short, no matter how presentational an event in my world is, when I observe it or communicate about it, it is inescapably discursive, inescapably a series of discrete bits. What does that mean? It means that the event in the real world and the event in my head are two utterly different things. The event "out there" is presentational, the event in my head is inevitably discursive. The event out there has no inherent order at all, while in my head the representation of that event has structure and order; not indeed the order that the event has, but the order that the process of my observation has given it. Further, it means that when I try to communicate my impression of real-world events, it must have an order and a structure; again, no structure that comes from the real world but only that structure that I give it.

But now, what is my purpose in communicating my impressions of an event? Is it not to recreate in the mind of my listener an impression of a given event similar (or isomorphic) to the one in my mind? But if the impression I communicate to someone else bears a structure and order not like the real event, but like the event as I observe it and as I communicate it, how can I hope to recreate the original event? The answer, of course, is I can't.

Since no matter how I describe an event, it is going to have some structure, some order, then I have to be careful to select a structure and order which will stimulate an impression in my listener's mind as close as possible to the one in my own.

In discussing the nature of descriptive patterns of organization we have used two words that have considerable significance: structure and order. It is now time to look a bit more closely at what we mean by structure and order. The word "order" implies that one thing comes after another in some sort of temporal or spatial sequence. The word "structure" implies that there is a reason above the order itself that explains why one thing follows another. The series "1, 3, 5, 7 . . . etc." has the order that the digit seven follows the digit five, which in turn follows the digit three. That fact alone would not be enough to predict that the next digit in the series would be nine. To make such a prediction would require that a person see through the order to the structure behind it: the series of consecutive odd numbers.

Another way of looking at the structure-order idea is that order refers to the details that will be put together in a pattern and that structure refers to the way in which those details will be combined into a whole.

Let us examine each of the types of descriptive patterns listed previously in this chapter and see how the structure-order concept fits in each.

Chronological

If I were to describe this day I might make the following list:

1. The clock radio awakened me at 6:30 A.M.
2. I began shaving at 7:02.
3. Breakfast began at 7:15 and included
   a. orange juice
   b. oatmeal
   c. bacon and eggs
   d. coffee
4. The children left for school at 7:35.

Etc.

All of this clearly has an order. The very fact that the list can be numbered consecutively indicates that. But it would be impossible to predict the next number of the series because there seems to be no consistent reason for ordering these numbers in the way that they are. There would be no reason at all for failing to include all of the events that occurred between 6:30 and 7:02. If, on the other hand, the list were presented as follows:

1. The clock radio awakened me at 6:30.
2. By 6:45 I had completed shaving.
3. By 7:00 the whole family was sitting down to breakfast.
   a. Precisely at 7:00 the orange juice was served.
   b. At 7:05 we began our oatmeal.
   c. At 7:10 the bacon and eggs were served.
4. By 7:15, having finished the coffee, we were ready for the final preparations in getting the children off to school.

You know very well that the next number of the series is the statement that the children left for school at 7:30. The order is not greatly different in this second list. But the structure is radically different. Not only can you predict the next member of the series but you can make some inferences about my purpose for writing the description, the quality of life in my family, and the relationships between me and my family. Clearly I was communicating an air of clock-like precision.

It is by the structure of your organizational pattern that you answer the questions: Why do you select the elements that you do and why do you arrange them in this order? In short, you communicate your purpose through the structure of your organizational pattern.

In the use of a chronological pattern, there ought clearly to be implied movement in a process toward the achievement of some goal. The details you select should be the rational steps necessary to achieve a clearly defined goal. These details should be arranged so that they reach a psychological climax in the achievement of the goal.

As an example, if I were to describe the freshman course I teach during the summer, I would probably do it in reference to the five weeks over which the course is taught. Some sort of organization like the following would probably result:

A. The first week is devoted to a study of communication theory aimed at an understanding of the internal processes that affect the communication of each individual. The processes covered are those of
1. Perception: how information is received into the human system;
2. Cognition: how this information is formed into concepts and stored;
3. Organization: how concepts are organized according to personality factors and by logical systems to direct behavior; and
4. Behavior: how we express our concept systems in behavioral choices both physically and verbally.
B. The second week is devoted to communication in groups or how the individual's communication system relates to those of others.
C. The third week deals with the processes of argumentation that may be used by the individual to lay out the alternatives of a choice for a second individual.
D. The fourth week then moves on to a study of the actual processes of choice that we call persuasion.
E. The fifth and final week is devoted entirely to a session in which the students put all these elements of communication together in an attempt to draw up methods of evaluating and grading themselves.

This is clearly a chronological pattern. The bare order of the pattern is given in the fact that one week follows another. The structure of the pattern, however, gives the pattern a purpose, a goal toward which it moves and a climax in which the goal is reached.

The chronological pattern of organization should probably be used whenever your subject can be looked at most conveniently and effectively as a process. Remember, such a pattern need not necessarily be tied to a rigid time sequence. The structure of the pattern is far more important. The purpose for which you are using the pattern should always be considered more important than the mere observance of strict time sequence.

Since when we look at reality we see it as a discursive process, then the natural way of describing our impression of an event is in some sort of chronological order. Since in the framework of the fundamental patterns of organization that aspect which deals with the factual content of an event is the data, then it is likely that when you expand on the data step you will do it by means of some sort of chronological approach.

Spatial

Perhaps a more sophisticated pattern of organization is the spatial. If we merely express our impressions the way they come to us, we would immediately fall into a chronological pattern. The stream of consciousness style of writing is fundamentally a chronological pattern. As such it is meant to duplicate the unstructured, unthought-out, and therefore unsophisticated workings of the human mind. When we try to sort out our impressions the first step beyond simple chronology is some ordering along spatial lines. Though we may have observed an event in a wholly haphazard way, when we relate that event to others we may wish to avoid the confusion we felt when we observed it. A spatial pattern of organization is one that relates an event by a consistently applied pattern of directions such as from one side to another, from top to bottom, from closer to us to farther from us.

As I sit here typing I can turn to the right and look through the slats of the Venetian blind at my office window. Immediately outside is a playground where some thirty or forty children are playing. These children live in the apartments immediately beyond the playground: the married student housing for our campus. Over toward the edge of the campus I can just see the roof of the freshman dormitories. Beyond this and over the tops of the trees I can trace the line of low-lying ridges that lie south of the city and run westward to the front range of the Rockies. And beyond these, rising above the distant haze, framed in the center of my window, is the rounded top of Pikes Peak.

The pattern of the paragraph above is spatial. The description moves from the typewriter, across the room to the window, through the window, and gradually into the distance. The structure of the paragraph implies that the climax will come when the description reaches the object toward which it is moving. The very fact that the description uses a consistent direction implies a moving toward something. It implies that I have already selected an end point and the structure of the paragraph gives that end-point suspense and climax.

It seems evident that the spatial pattern of organization is a far more sophisticated, far more carefully contrived mode of presenting material than the chronological. It must be carefully thought out. All of the elements must be put together in such a way that they contribute to the force of the climax. In the example above, for instance, the fact that there are thirty or forty children playing in the playground really has very little to do with the point of the description. The smallness of the children might contrast with the largeness of the central point of the description, but other than that, this element might well have been left out. The fact that the buildings beyond the playground are married student housing was to some degree irrelevant. The purpose of the description is embodied in the movement of my eyes from the typewriter little more than a foot away to the top of Pikes Peak well over eighty miles from here.

The value of this pattern of organization lies in its emphasis on the object or element toward which the description moves. It creates the impression that the last object of the description is somehow the most important or impressive and therefore should be remembered.

Relative-Spatial

The relative-spatial pattern of organization does not organize the description of an event according to a consistent set of directions, but rather by a consistent comparative principle. If I say that the three tallest manmade structures in the world are the Empire State Building, the Chrysler Building, and the RCA Building, I would be organizing the description by a relative-spatial pattern. The order involved in this description is simply the enumeration of the three tallest buildings. The structure of that order is that the three be arranged from the tallest of the three downward. If I should say that the four largest cities in the United States are Los Angeles, Chicago, Philadelphia, and New York, this too would be a relative-spatial pattern. The structure would be enumeration from west to east. Listing the three means of public transportation as air, rail, and auto would be to list according to speed. To say rail, air, and auto could be a listing by passenger capacity. Any organization, then, by relative size, height, weight, position, or motion can be considered a relative-spatial pattern of organization.

Relative-Perceptual

This pattern of organization, in a sense, overlaps with the previous one. Generally speaking, we detect spatial distinctions by means of perceptual differences. A relative difference in brightness is interpreted as a relative difference in distance. The difference in the two modes of organization lies in the observer's assumptions. If the observer infers that the perceptual difference he detects in himself is due to a real difference in the objects he is viewing and he reports that difference as being in the object, then he is using the relative-spatial or spatial pattern of organization. If, on the other hand, he does not make this inferential leap and assumes only that his perception of objects is different and organizes his report according to the internal differences, he is then using the relative-perceptual pattern.

Patterns which arrange elements according to loudness, brightness, hardness, sharpness, clarity, or any other perceived distinctions between objects or events are relative-perceptual patterns. If, for instance, I should talk of the instruments in an orchestra, I might very well discuss them in terms of relative pitch, starting with the double bass, tuba, contra-bassoon, and maybe contra-clarinet, moving up the scale to the violin, cornet, flute, and piccolo. If I were talking about the paintings of Van Gogh, I might arrange them in terms of his color periods from the soft blues and green to the violent reds, yellows, and oranges.

Summary

In using any of these descriptive patterns of organization, one primary factor of structure must be remembered. The structure used in organizing must be consistently applied. There is nothing that confuses a listener more than switching a structure in mid-description. There must be nothing in the organization which conflicts with the purpose of that organization. The organizational pattern you choose must have a clear, specific purpose and that purpose must be carried through the whole of it. In the example of the description of the view from my window, several elements were present that conflicted with the purpose of the description. This inconsistency in structure should be avoided.

LOGICAL PATTERNS OF ORGANIZATION

We will discuss two classes of logical patterns, one based on the analysis-synthesis concept, the other based on the cause-effect relationship. You may have noticed an interesting fact already. In the very naming of two classes of logical patterns, we find the fundamental nature of any logical pattern. Let's explore this nature briefly before we go on to discuss the two classes.

The very existence of a language implies a logic and any logic requires a language for its expression. Any language may be described as a group of visible or audible symbols which stand for objects in reality or mental concepts that people have about reality. Concepts about reality or words standing for reality have a peculiar nature. There are only two things you can do with a symbol when you apply it to an object: you can assert that a symbol does stand for that object or you can assert that the symbol does not stand for that object. Indeed, you may qualify either of these assertions. You can say that 95 per cent of the time A is B. You can say that under conditions x and y, A is never B. However qualified, you must assert either that symbol A stands for object B in part or wholly, or you must assert that symbol A does not stand wholly or in part for object B. It makes no difference that the language or the logic may have nothing to do with the object; what does matter is that language binds you to a polarized way of looking at the world.

When Aristotle studied this dichotomous quality of language he postulated three laws of thought. What these laws say is that if you want to use language and make sense, you have to play the game with certain rules. Violate the rules and your language no longer can be depended on. This is not to say that Aristotle thought the world of our senses could always be fitted into dichotomous categories, but that formal logic is dependable only to the degree that these rules can be obeyed. Take his first rule, the rule of identity. It is usually written: A equals A, or A is identical to A. What this means is that if you are going to make sense with your language, make sure that when you use a word that refers to a particular object at one time in a conversation, it means the same thing when you use it again. In other words, if you use the same word twice in a conversation, as much as possible it ought to mean the same thing. This does not mean that objects don't change. This is not to say that an object or an event is always what you say it is. It only means that when you violate the rule, people have a hard time following you.

The second rule is the law of noncontradiction: A does not equal non-A. Here is the heart of this peculiar nature of language. This law says that a thing cannot be both A and non-A at the same time. If your language is going to make sense to someone else you had better make sure that when you use a word to refer to a particular object, you don't use the negative of that word later to refer to the same object. Imagine the feelings of a girl talking to her doctor if that doctor said, "Well, although you are pregnant, you shouldn't worry about it, since you aren't really pregnant." That sentence does not make sense. The girl cannot determine her behavior from that point on until she knows for certain whether she is or she isn't. In her view, she has to be one or the other.

The third of Aristotle's three rules follows from the others. It is the law of the excluded middle: B is either A or non-A. Suppose we let A represent this typewriter. Then everything else in the world can be considered non-A, that is, nothing else in this world is *this* typewriter. All right, let's take some object in the world and call it B. Call the pencil on my desk B. Is it A or non-A? It is clearly not the typewriter; since the typewriter equals A and everything else is non-A (non-this typewriter), and therefore it must be non-A. How about the shift key on this typewriter? That is clearly part of the typewriter so it must be A. When you are talking about typewriters and pregnant girls then this law gives us no trouble. A girl is definitely either pregnant or not pregnant, an object is clearly either this typewriter or it is not this typewriter. The trouble comes when we ask questions like: Is this action just or unjust? Is this man a thief or is he not a thief? Is this electron a wave or is it not a wave?

The point here is that the world cannot be absolutely divided. Strictly speaking, everything is changing and therefore becoming what it is not. Because we can give a name to something we cannot think that we have captured its nature for all time. The point is that language with its adherence to Aristotle's three laws of thought is merely a convenient fiction. It is something that we accept as a convention, but know that the reality is different. Language, mathematics, symbolic logic, or traditional logic are all conventional systems that have no necessary relationship with the real world. They make us comfortable when we use them because they give us a sense (sometimes a false sense) of security and stability.

But how does this relate to the logical patterns of organization? A logical pattern of organization is a fiction that we impose upon our world in order to make it more manageable in our language. That is, when we deal with something logically we behave rigorously and consistently not because the reality we are dealing with is rigorous or consistent, but rather because our language makes more sense to us when we behave that way. Somtimes this behavior may prevent us from seeing something important in the thing we are observing, but the logic at least makes us comfortable with that reality. For instance, there are people among us who cannot tolerate the ambiguity of saying that our present condition as a nation in the world is the result of many international and national forces working together in a complex way. Because this ambiguity makes us so uncomfortable we invent the logic of a conspiracy theory of world affairs. If we do not like the world situation, it's because of the Communist conspiracy, Soviet expansionism, Monolithic Communism, the Big Lie. If we do not like the direction our nation is taking at home, we blame it on Communist subversion. It's not our fault or the result of complex events, it is simply the fault of the Communist, or the Jew, or the pushy "nigger," or whoever else happens to be the devil at that moment.

We use logical patterns not because they fit reality, but only because with them we can deal with reality more comfortably. Sometimes they can help us look at reality more objectively, to be less prone to emotional snap judgments.

We will limit our discussion here to two classes of logical organizations. These are probably the most common and the most useful. The first is that class of patterns that may be characterized by the polarized concept of analysis-synthesis, the second is that class of patterns based on the cause-effect relationship.

Analysis-Synthesis

Simply stated, analysis means the process of breaking something apart while synthesis means the process of putting something together. This is a pretty fundamental idea. We have the feeling that everything can be broken down into its parts or, having the parts, a whole can be put together from them. The Greeks in examining this idea asked themselves what happens when you analyze things into smaller and smaller parts and they came to the concept of the atom, the indivisible basic particle. Modern physics has discovered that what we had called the atom is really not the indivisible particle as had been thought. There are yet smaller particles. In fact they may not even be particles but rather special conditions of a universal field.

The example given in the introduction to this section was the description of a machine as an analytic-synthetic pattern. The machine may be considered first as a whole and then in terms of its parts. A painting can be analyzed in terms of its constituent parts: color, line, and form. This is a logical analysis. Can you conceive of a line without color, or a form without line? Of course not. None of these three elements can exist without the others. You see a painting as a whole, without any distinctions. The concepts of color, line, and form are artificial categories created to help us deal with the object. Another way of looking at the same picture might be in terms of figure and ground. Again this is an artificial creation that helps deal with aspects of the painting that perhaps would have escaped us had we used the color-line-form categories. The three distinctions made between descriptive, logical, and valuative patterns of organization are of the same nature. Types of organization might be classified in any number of ways. I use this one because it makes the most sense to me; I am most comfortable with it. The point here is that no message can exist without some sort of order. Since your message will have some order anyway, you ought to choose an order that makes as much sense as possible to you. Hopefully it will also make sense to the listener. Since the analytic-synthetic patterns of viewing the world are so familiar to most people, it is likely that by using them you will make sense to your listener.

One more example of the analytic-synthetic pattern may help to make it clear. Motion is extremely complex. In the real world there is no such thing as uniform, straight-line motion. How then does the mathematician or the physicist talk about motion and make sense? Clearly, to talk about

the indistinguishable, undifferentiable real motion of a particle makes
no sense at all, so the mathematician (like Descartes) creates a fiction,
the fiction of component motions. Instead of considering the real motion
of the particle in space, he talks about the three component motions
along the x, y, and z axes of a totally imaginary frame of reference.
Analysis consists of breaking down the real motion into its fictional
component parts. Synthesis consists of the prediction of positions along
the line by putting the parts together again (for instance, the prediction
of the impact point of a ballistic missile).

In an analytic-synthetic pattern, then, the parts into which a whole
is going to be divided are stated and then each part is considered separately. The following is an example:

A. In giving grades the teacher should consider the student's grasp of
information and his application of that information.
  1. Probably the best way to deal with information is through an objective test.
  2. Probably the best method of judging application is to observe the
  student in free discussion with his peers.

This brief outline is no less reasonable for the fact that in actual
practice no human being could distinguish between information held
and application of that information. Isn't a test a form of application?
The point is that because I can separate two aspects of the student's
"knowledge" I am more comfortable in dealing with the reality. Not only
that, but my listener will make more sense out this message.

Note that the pattern in the example is primarily analytical; that is,
a whole is taken and divided. A synthetic pattern would take the parts
and derive a whole from them. Unfortunately, methods of outlining are
all analytical in nature and so on the surface both the analytic and the
synthetic look the same. The following would be an example of what
could be a synthetic pattern.

A. Grades are a detriment to a speech class; they thwart the very goals
of such a class, for
  1. They encourage the student to imitate the instructor, and since
  2. The goal of the course is not imitation but the development of
  individual style.

I said this could be synthetic. If the speaker, in giving the message,
developed points 1 and 2 and from them derived claim A, this would
be a synthetic pattern. Another name would be an inductive pattern.
If, on the other hand, he stated the conclusion first and then provided
the data and the warrant, it would be an analytic pattern. Another name
for this would be a deductive pattern. As a matter of fact, since the
speaker had the conclusion in his head already, even though it might

have appeared inductive, in reality the speaker's thinking was deductive. A true induction can only occur when the conclusion is unknown until derived from the data.

Notice how we have talked about two types of analytic-synthetic patterns. The first one dealt with objects like machines and paintings and the motion of particles and divided them into their component parts or from the parts derived the object. These are the analyses and syntheses based on the part-whole relationship. The second type dealt with the making of judgments, with conclusions and premises. These are the deductive and inductive patterns. Another type of pattern is that based on the general-particular relationship. These state or deal with a general class and then speak about the particulars in the class. An example:

The three largest automobile manufacturers in the United States are General Motors, Ford, and Chrysler.*

Another example is the one that this chapter uses:

A. Descriptive patterns of organization
   1. Chronological
   2. Spatial
   3. Relative-spatial
   4. Relative-perceptual
B. Logical patterns of organization
   1. Analytic-synthetic
   2. Cause-effect
C. Valuational patterns of organization

A fourth type of analytic-synthetic pattern is that based on the relationship between abstractions and their concrete examples. For instance:

The keystones of our legal system are trial by a jury of a man's peers, due process, and the presumption that a man is innocent until he is proved guilty.

Cause-Effect

The cause-effect relationship is really a special case of the analytic-synthetic class of pattern. In general, the relationships dealt with in the analytic-synthetic patterns are left somewhat vague. Specifics are related to generalities by "logical inclusion", parts are related to wholes by some sort of physical inclusion. Superficially, at least, the relationship of a cause to its effects or an effect to its causes (in multiple causation) is

---

*Notice that in the very structure of this pattern is implied a relative-spatial pattern by size.

similar. But on a deeper level there is more to this relationship. The analytic-synthetic pattern is based on the assumption of divisibility in the world of ideas as well as the physical world. The cause-effect pattern is based on a far more consequential assumption: that of the absolute determination of an effect by its antecedent causes. This assumption is so fundamentally a part of our thinking structure that we tend almost automatically to fall into this pattern. Superficially it is handled much the same way as the analytic-synthetic patterns. The outlines will look much the same. But when you say that there is a cause-effect relationship between a major point in an outline and the subpoints following it, you claim far more. We have talked about the criteria for judging whether A is the cause of B in a previous chapter. Before you imply or state that relationship in your subsidiary or fundamental patterns of organization, you must be able to support it with sufficient data and a reasonable warrant.

Summary

It should be clear that the logical patterns of organization will fit anywhere in the fundamental patterns. They may be used to explicate data that cannot be handled descriptively. They may be used to back the warrant. Wherever possible, the speaker should use descriptive patterns. The more logical the patterns that are used, the more the speaker is moving away from the reality he is dealing with and into his own imagination.

VALUATIONAL PATTERNS OF ORGANIZATION

We will deal with valuational patterns briefly. In all such patterns the speaker says that in the list of things, ideas, or events that I am dealing with, *to me*, A is more valuable than B and B is more valuable than C. All this pattern does is structure an order of ideas presented in terms of the intensity of the speaker's feelings about them, either from the most intense to the least, or the other way around.

You might say that such patterns should be avoided. I would disagree. As logical or as factual as we might try to be, ultimately all really important questions come down to a matter of values. Some of you might be thinking right now, if it comes to a choice between fighting in a way I think is wrong and going to jail, I'd rather go to jail. This is a valuational pattern and it is one you cannot escape from. One of these two alternatives has to be placed first. If there are three alternatives, we must rank them, and the determination of which comes first is a matter of values and morals.

Valuational patterns are not difficult to use. The question is knowing when to use them. I would say that they should be avoided as much as possible, but that when the real question at issue is one of values, be ready to explain your value system as clearly and as fully as you can. It is sometimes said that values, like tastes, cannot be argued. This is not true. They can and should be argued. Ultimately they will be accepted or rejected on two grounds: do the consequences that follow from accepting these values seem good to me? and, do I respect the man who holds them?

Notice what I am saying. The valuational pattern of organization merely determines in which order you will place a number of valued alternatives. The important point is that when you do, you have in effect asserted a claim, namely that this is the order that should be given them. You should then be ready to support that assertion by the statement of data and warrant.

SUMMARY

There are three subsidiary patterns of organization which may be used to modify or support the fundamental patterns of organization. It seems to me that one proposition should be asserted from this chapter. You cannot avoid having some order when you say two or more things. There then ought to be a reason and structure for your organizational pattern. If you don't have a reason it is an indication that you are confused, and you can be certain that your listener will be confused. You must be able to give a reason for putting one thing before another or relating two things the way you do. We've said it before: you cannot depend on your listener being any less reasonable than you are.

EXERCISES

1. Develop the issues for a speech on a simple central idea.
2. Develop four different ways (patterns of organization) in which to present the data. Show how and why you use each.
3. Develop four different ways in which to present the warrant and its backing. Show how and why you use each.
4. Develop four different ways in which to argue the reservation. Show how and why you use each.

READINGS

On the presentational and discursive distinction see:

LANGER, SUSANNE, *Philosophy in a New Key* (New York: Mentor Books), 1961.

Chapter 7

THE MESSAGE ITSELF

When Aristotle dealt with this subject some 2200 years ago he intimated that all a speaker really has to do is to state his case and prove it—he could, that is, except for the sorry state of the audience. We have so far dealt with the structure of ideas and the materials which directly support the central idea. Unless the listener is exceptionally intelligent, more is necessary. The idea has to be suitably introduced to the listener, the parts must be appropriately tied together, and the message must achieve some kind of psychologically and aesthetically pleasing closure. These, then, are the three things this chapter will deal with: introduction, transition, and conclusion.

INTRODUCTION

An introduction is simply the way in which a speaker gets a person ready to listen to his ideas. Proper preparation involves three things. First, the speaker must know precisely what he is going to talk about before he puts his introduction together. Second, the speaker must know how ready the audience is to listen. Third, he must know how ready they need to be.

What constitutes readiness to listen? Here, too, there are three elements that may be considered. There will be in any particular situation some physical conditions which either work to discourage or encourage a person's listening. This provides a physical set toward listening.* Second, there is a psychological set that will influence listening. Finally, there is an intellectual set. In the first part of this chapter, then, we will discuss these three sets that influence listening; the physical, the psycho-

---

*A set is a readiness to act in a particular way. A runner in the starting block has a physical set toward the act of running, a psychological set toward the sound of the gun.

logical, and the intellectual. In each case we will examine what the speaker ought to know about his listener and how the introduction should be structured to deal with that knowledge. We will not deal with the question of the speaker's own understanding of his point because preparation of the message has been covered earlier.

In the analysis that follows we will be dealing with factors of the speaking situation that are often considered beyond the control and therefore the interest of the speaker. The question we will be addressing is whether we can judge the mental state of a listener from the situation in which he is located and from the non-verbal cues that may be present. I believe that to a certain extent we can. But we can do it only to the degree that we pay attention to things that before may have been beneath our notice. It is for this reason that we will go into such detail in describing elements of the speaking situation.

Physical Set

You would not expect to have people listen eagerly to a lecturer holding forth in the medial strip of a superhighway. You would probably even have a difficult time catching an audience in the middle of a sidewalk. In both cases the physical situation is one designed for motion and provides little opportunity for the centering of attention on a speaker. If you were committed to speaking to a group on a street, the corner might be better because the motion, at least, would be more in your direction and you would have a longer time to capture attention. A plaza or square might be better still, and comparatively speaking a park might almost be considered ideal. A person in a park is probably a better listener because he is not generally committed to motion. He is rather open to some leisure and often to sources of stimulation away from his direction of travel.

The more physically committed to motion away from or tangential to a speaker, the less likely he is to pay attention to that speaker. This commitment involves four factors: proximity, direction, motion, and noise.*

Generally speaking, the closer a listener is to a speaker, the more committed he is to listening to that speaker. Inevitably, if a person does not want to listen he will move away from the speaker. The speaker can tell how much a person wants to listen to him by how close a person sits. The fact that most auditoriums have entrances in the back is significant here. Other factors being equal, the farther forward a person walks, the

---

*The word "noise" here is used in its engineering sense of "interfering or irrelevent energy" like motion, color, touch, or smell that does not relate to the message.

more physical energy he exerts, the more committed he is. There is a psychological factor involved here too. If there are people in the auditorium, the more he walks forward, the more the listener exposes himself to the observation of others. You can almost make the judgment that a person who walks to the front row when other seats are available is willing to commit himself to becoming involved in the speaker.

The speaker can estimate the commitment of a listener by his posture. A posture of leaning back or away from a speaker will tell that speaker that psychologically at least this man wants to get away. A posture of leaning forward indicates a high degree of commitment—such a person is ready to listen to you.

It is not by chance that churches generally fill up from the back, movie-houses fill from the middle, and high intensity political rallies fill up from the front.

Auditoria are generally fan-shaped, rows of seats are in shallow semi-circles, and each seat faces the speaker's platform directly. Even the ceiling and walls move down and in to center on the speaker. The whole physical environment is aimed at the source of stimulation. The whole room says, "Pay attention."

Generally speaking, the more the room does this, the more committed will be the people who sit there listening to the speaker. In older style auditoria where the seats are arranged in a rigid rectangle, if there are more seats than people and if the audience is intensely interested in the speaker, the audience will occupy the seats that form a fan-shape, with the speaker where the handle of the fan would be. Not only that, but the people on the sides will be turned, physically, in their seats to face the speaker directly.

When people are interested in what a speaker has to say they will physically respond: they will tend to move closer to the sources of stimuli they like, trust, enjoy and they will move away from sources which they dislike, mistrust, and are irritated by. Generally when the movements of a listener are away from or tangential to the speaker, that speaker may infer that the listener is reacting negatively. Generally when the movements of a listener are inward toward the speaker, that speaker may infer that the listener is reacting positively. This is particularly true of those movements that the listener is not likely to consciously control, like the movement of the eyes, the positions of the fingers, the position of the feet.

Finally, the absence of other interfering stimuli will tend to make a listener pay more attention. Modern auditoria are built very plainly. There is generally no distracting decoration that would fall in even the peripheral vision of the audience and is certainly never above or behind the speaker. Seats are generally arranged, as we noted before, in shallow semicircles. If they were deep semicircles the movements of the other members of the audience would be too distracting. On the other hand, a shallow semicircle puts enough others in the periphery of the listener's vision to give him the impression that others are listening to the speaker. This in turn puts social pressure on the listener to listen more attentively.

The extreme limitation of irrelevant stimuli to the point where the only stimuli possible are those from the speaker in effect results in hypnosis of the listener. If a person were deprived of all stimulation except that from one source, that person would become absolutely dependent upon that source. He would make no choices, have no motives, feel no feelings except those that the source approved, because that source would soon become the whole world, the only environment for the person. This could result in a total loss of freedom and even individuality.

When a person is committed to listening to a speaker, he will seek to limit noise. He will limit his vision as much as possible to the speaker. He will seek as much stimulation as he can get from the speaker, like moving as close as possible, leaning forward, cupping his ear, shading his eyes, and even reaching out and touching. The extremely committed listener will become angry at, hostile to, anything that distracts him.

There are, then, environmental factors which will make it impossible for a person to listen; prevent him from choosing to listen. There are also environmental factors which will make it impossible for a person not to listen; prevent him from choosing not to listen. Brainwashing techniques are the extreme case of such environmental control. And there are factors that will leave him free to choose either to listen or not to listen. The question of how much a speaker has a right to limit or control the choice of a listener is left to the last chapter. Here we are dealing only with how the environment affects listening behavior.

The degree of commitment a listener has to listening to a speaker directly influences his physical behavior in the presence of the speaker. Thus, the speaker can, and indeed must, judge how he comes across to a listener by observing his physical responses. Any speaker who does not know how a listener is receiving him and his message is either perceptually handicapped, dead, or just plain stupid.

What can a speaker do in an introduction to command the physical attention of his listener? Well, first, he can try to directly control or alter the physical environment. He can find out, if necessary by asking, whether his listener can hear. If a light makes it difficult for a listener to see, have the light turned off or blocked. If a listener cannot see, move so he can. If possible, have the listener move closer or move closer to the audience.

If there are interfering stimuli that you can remove, do so. If they cannot be removed and it is clear that people cannot avoid paying attention to them, mention them, explain the effect they will have, and suggest ways of overcoming them. If nothing else the listener will recognize a concern on your part for them and will tend to respond favorably to you and become more committed to listening.

Most effective is the kind of introduction that seeks a specific feedback, overt response, from the listener. This asks him to make a commitment of physical energy. However, if you force a listener into making overt responses or physical commitments that he really would rather avoid, he may then resent you. You have thereby lost a listener. Always leave the listener with a real choice so that if he does choose to respond it will be because he wanted to.

Psychological Set

What I mean by psychological set is an attitudinal predisposition to react to a message in a particular way. The listener may be so predisposed to react because of attitudes toward the speaker, because of attitudes to the speaker's subject, or because of attitudes toward the situation. If a man's boss sends him to a speech that he does not really want to hear, then that man will resent the situation and he will direct that hostility at the speaker and his message. If a student is required to take a course and he resents the course or the requirement, he will also resent the teacher and what he has to say. The speaker must know the situation and generally why his listener is there. If there is a strong attitude against hearing the message, then sometimes the speaker should deal with it openly and objectively. Ultimately the best way for the speaker to handle such strong attitudes is to talk about them as frankly and honestly as he can. If the attitude is *not* so terribly strong that it will make the listener reject the speaker and his ideas immediately, then perhaps the speaker can win the kind of attention that he wants by indirection.

There are three types of attention. There is involuntary attention which a person pays to stimuli that are just so overpowering that he physically cannot resist. You are reading in a deathly still library and someone behind you suddenly screams. You are in a darkened room and a bright light flashes. You are a stranger at a busy airport and somebody calls your name. You are looking at a painting in an art gallery and you catch a quick movement in your peripheral vision. All of these are examples of involuntary attention. It would take actual and even extreme physical effort to *avoid* paying attention to such things. This kind of stimulus catches attention but tends not to be able to hold it for very long unless the nature of the stimulus keeps changing. Change in itself demands some degree of involuntary attention.

A second type of attention is voluntary attention. This type of attention is that which we feel obliged to pay to a source of stimulation. We have been taught to be polite and not to show boredom in the presence of those speaking to us—we therefore try to show interest and be attentive. We try to listen to the minister no matter how dull he is. This kind of attention takes real physical effort to maintain. Usually it does not last long, is highly intermittent, and will tend to fade and disappear if not supported by some other form of attention.

The third kind of attention is habitual attention. This is the attention that is not so overwhelming that we cannot resist it, but at the same time it does not require a great deal of effort to maintain it. This is the kind of attention we give to hobbies or people that we like very much, or music that we enjoy, or subjects that fascinate us. We have learned to enjoy particular kinds of stimulation and we actively seek it and can maintain our attention to it with little or no effort.

It is likely, then, that at the start of the speaker's message, unless there are strong physical or psychological sets toward or against listening, that the listener will be paying voluntary attention. This kind of attention is an effort to maintain. It therefore follows that the speaker wants to create a more favorable kind of attention. He has two choices: involuntary or habitual.

The popular nineteenth-century preacher, Henry Ward Beecher, faced a particularly difficult audience. It was a hot night. The auditorium was jammed and stuffy. People were irritated by the heat and a long, boring introduction. In short, no one was paying attention. Beecher came to the speaker's stand, took off his coat, removed his tie, wiped his forehead with a handkerchief, and said, "It's Goddam hot tonight!" The whole audience gasped at once. There was a shocked, unbelieving silence. Then Beecher said, "That's what I heard someone say here tonight." And from that point moved into a sermon against profanity. That introduction demanded instant, involuntary attention.

So did another. A girl walked up to the front of a speech class, climbed onto a chair, stepped up to the top of the teacher's desk, and lifted her skirt as high as she could. That too commanded instant, involuntary attention. The difference was that Beecher immediately could convert his listener's attention into real interest. So could the girl, but not also get the point she intended across. She had nowhere *reasonable* to go next.

If you choose to get attention by doing something striking, something that aims at involuntary attention, you have to be sure it does not go so far that there is no way to get your listener back to your point. You have probably seen speakers who use some sort of striking technique and then continue from one striking thing to the next until you are bored and may even feel sorry and embarrassed for the speaker. Dirty jokes have a tendency to put speakers in that kind of a bind.

If then you use some sort of striking introduction, make sure it has relevance to your point. Sooner or later you must create habitual attention, and the sooner you do it the better.

You may well ask how does a speaker create habitual attention, particularly if the message has no immediate interest to the listener? There is no subject so remote that no connection can be found to the real interests of the audience. (If you have found such a subject then you might well question whether you should use it.) Two things are required: you must know what the interests of the listener are and then you must connect your idea to it. In Chapter 4 we discussed material used as illustration and talked about what makes people identify with the speaker and his message. A review of this would help here. For instance, vivid description or narration will tend to draw attention from the listener. Such material can be used in the introduction if relevant to your point.

Another way to gain habitual attention is by creating identification with yourself. This is often called "establishing common ground." That is, what does this listener have in common with me that will lead him to accept my idea? Reference to such material should create a real interest. A warning here. A speaker cannot safely fake a common ground. Either find a real community of interest with the listener or do not use this kind of introduction.

Intellectual Set

You must adapt your idea to what the audience can intellectually comprehend. If you are a high-energy particle physicist speaking in your area of expertise to a grammar school PTA, you must adapt a great deal. If you are a grade school teacher talking about the problems of teaching addition to first graders before a group of theoretical mathematicians, you must also adapt. When we talked before about choosing subjects, we pointed out that if the gap is too big to bridge, then forget the subject.

If the speaker is on the high end of the gap and the listener does not have the intellectual tools to understand the speaker's point, the speaker can go two ways. He can either give the listener the tools to understand or he can make his subject fit the listener's ability. The first choice involves some sort of explanatory instructions. This will include definitions of important terms, criteria for making judgments, things to look for as the speaker goes along, a summary of the points to be covered, and most of all a real opportunity to ask questions when needed.

Fitting the subject to the listener's ability is more difficult. An introduction here would seek to show how the speaker's central idea satisfies some need or needs of the audience, would allay fears that the listener might have of the subject's incomprehensibility, and would seek as many effective analogies as the speaker could find in the experience of the listener. This choice can be particularly dangerous. If the speaker assumes the stupidity of the listener, the listener will feel hurt and angry and will do everything he can to reject the speaker's message. If, on the other hand, the speaker assumes a bit too much of his listener, the listener will tend to be pleased and make real efforts to come up to the speaker's estimate of him. In short, anything less than a genuine respect and liking for your listener is likely to turn him off toward you.

Once you have gotten started in the message, there are still problems of relating to the listener. The major one is that of transition.

TRANSITION

It is easy for a speaker who has something to say and knows his subject well to see connections where the listener may be unable to see them. The speaker hopefully has thought out his central idea. He has painstakingly worked out the support for that idea. In his mind he sees how the message hangs together. For him the idea is a gem and the message is a perfectly matched setting. It is sometimes a shock to the speaker to receive the feedback afterward that the setting was in pieces and the stone wasn't even there.

The only judge of whether a message was well put together is the listener. If he could not follow, then the message was not followable no matter how good it seemed to the speaker. Either there was nothing there to follow or the speaker did not lead the listener from point to point. If it is the first, this chapter will do the speaker little good. We might be able to help the second problem. The difficulty in that second instance is one of transitioning.

Every point should be tied to the one before and the one after by some appropriate transition. This rule requires conscious and careful attention because a good transition must fulfill certain characteristics.

First, a good transition should summarize the point preceding. Second, it should establish the evaluational, logical, temporal, or spatial relationship between the preceding and following ideas. Third, it must preview the following point.

Transitions can be brief or very long. For instance:

> What we have done up to this point is enumerate what I think are the goals of this course. None of us would now include in the course some exercise or technique which would thwart those goals, at least not knowingly. But that's just what we have done. Using grades does just that. Let me show you how.

This is a rather long transition, the kind of transition that might be used in a carefully argued logical argument. Let's look at it analytically to see if it fulfills the three functions of a transition. That first sentence tells the listener that he has just heard a list of goals for the course. According to this sentence it was a bare enumeration and therefore had very little internal cohesiveness. In short, it is warning the listener that he was not expected to get from the previous point anything more than a number of relatively isolated items, and that if he got no more than this, he was not to worry. The first function seems quite well handled.

The next two sentences in the transition show how the two points are connected. By implication it establishes the principle that a course ought to be designed to fulfill its goals and that nothing should be done in the course that works against their fulfillment. In contrast, then, to what would be reasonable behavior in conducting a course is the way in which we actually behave. What follows is a violation of the principle just laid down, in that what follows shows how a method or technique used in the course thwarts the goals we have just enumerated. This transition, then, shows definitely how the points are connected.

The third function of the transition is handled in the last two sentences. The first of the two sentences indicates what it is that thwarts the goals of the course and the subject of the next point. The last sentence indicates that the purpose of the point following is to explain how it is that using grades violates the goals of the course, and both of them together imply that the point will show how each and every goal will be dealt with. This seems to be a complete transition.

As I said, some transitions are very short. For instance:

> therefore

This single word also fulfills all the functions of the transition. First, it indicates that what preceded was the ground (data and/or warrant). Second, it indicates that the following point is related to the first by logical implication. Third, it indicates that what follows is the claim of the argument. You could not ask for anything more than that. The only difficulty might be that if the listener was inattentive, he might have missed it.

Here is another:

and

Very short. But still fulfilling the function. When the speaker uses this he is saying three things: (1) I am in the middle of a list of at least two things and the preceding point is a member of that list. (2) I am now moving from one member of the list to another and they are related as equals, coordinate members in a group of equally important members. (3) The next member of the list is about to follow and (if I have used a rising and falling inflection or if no *and* came between the other members of the list) this is the last one.

The use of such transitions as "and," "next," then," and the like are generally a mark of childish speech. A child will generally not recognize the complex interrelationships existing between the things he is saying, and so he will often connect long strings of complex ideas or events coordinately (with "and"), or temporally (with "next" or "then") when really the relationships are far more complex. In most cases your thoughts are in more complex relationships than merely coordinate or temporal and therefore deserve far more complex transitions. When you use an inappropriate transition which fails to identify the precise relationship between your points, you are almost sure to lose your listener. You have given him a bridge across the gap between your points that just will not bear his weight.

The key to using good transitions is a simple one. Know precisely how your ideas are related and then spell out that relationship for your listener.

CONCLUSION

The conclusion is acceptable if it is appropriate. The speaker can determine what sort of a conclusion to use by asking the question of himself: what does my listener need? Let's list some of the things you can do and discuss in each case what conditions make it appropriate.

Plea for Action

This is simply asking or demanding that the listener do something. "Vote *No* on Amendment Fourteen!" "Sign up at your local recruiting station!" "Buy Clairol and see!" "Help a child today!" All of these are pleas for some sort of action. When the point of your message was that something ought to be done, then it is always appropriate to ask the listener to do it. The way in which you ask ought to be gauged to what you perceive the audience's acceptance of your idea has been. If you are speaking to the American Legion asking them to support the elimination of the draft, then it would be inappropriate (unless you have wholly changed them) to ask them to picket the Pentagon. You might reasonably ask them to "think about it." Review Chapter 2. Just as the state of the listener determines what your central idea should be, just so the immediate state of the listener determines what you can ask him to do. Though you can plan alternative pleas, you cannot really tell what will be appropriate until you see how the listener responds. Then do what seems appropriate.

Summary

The summary conclusion is extremely valuable, particularly at the end of complex, intellectually loaded messages. A brief summary recapitulating the structure of your idea will fix that idea more firmly in the consciousness of the listener. Make sure it is *brief, clear,* and *faithful* to the structure you used. The summary is almost never out of place. In emotionally loaded messages, a summary, if used at all, should be very brief and aimed sharply at the emotional change you are intending. Wherever it is used a summary brings a sense of closure and completion.

Epitome

The epitome conclusion is the gem on velvet, it's the moral at the end of the fable, it's the few words that say it all. It's the kind of thing that you remember long after the speaker has finished. You can list a dozen. Here are a few:

Now abideth faith, hope, love; these three. But the greatest of these is love.

Liberty and union, one and inseparable, now and forever.

Give me liberty or give me death!

With malice toward none, with charity for all, with firmness in the right as God gives us to see the right, let us strive on to finish the work we are in, to bind up the nation's wounds, to care for him who shall have borne the battle and for his widow and his orphan, to do all which may achieve and cherish a just and lasting peace among ourselves and with all nations.

In brief, an epitome conclusion is one which restates the central idea in a memorable way. It is in the form of a slogan, or an epigram. It places before the listener a clear and beautiful wording of what you were telling him all along.

Go thou and do likewise.

SUMMARY

The listener has to be made ready to listen. He has to be guided from point to point. He has to be left with a sense of closure. All this is true most of the time. However, if you have something that the listener really needs, if he knows he needs it and is sure he will get it from you, and if you really give it to him, you can then forget everything we've said here. In such a circumstance it makes no difference how you say it as long as you give the listener what he needs. All you have to do then is say it.

Exercises

1. Go through this chapter and select two introductions used by the author in the text. Analyze and criticize them.
2. Go through this chapter and select two conclusions. Analyze and criticize them.
3. Take the section of this chapter on "Transition."
   a. Outline it. Include central ideas and all main points.
   b. Describe and criticize the introduction and conclusion.
   c. Select three good transitions and tell why they are good.
   d. Select three bad transitions and tell why they are bad.

Chapter 8

PREPARING FOR DELIVERY

At first it may seem strange to be dealing with matters of delivery in a book on the content and organization of speeches. The point of view adopted here, however, is that the structure of the speech is never set until the speech is over. The moment the speaker can no longer change, can no longer adapt to changing circumstances, the speech is dead.

In this chapter we will not be discussing specific matters of delivery, voice, gesture, style. The delivery, however, directly reflects the preparation. Preparation must therefore include the choice of a mode of delivery, the choice of a mode of practice, and specific considerations of adaptation to particular speaking situations.

MODES OF DELIVERY

The modes of delivery available to the speaker range from the totally impromptu on one end of a continuum to the recorded and played back on the other end. No matter what mode of delivery the speaker chooses, he will find that the methods of developing content and organization discussed in this book will be invaluable to him. Let's consider several of the modes of delivery and see how content and organization are adapted to fit each situation.

Impromptu

Impromptu speaking is unprepared. You are sitting comfortably at the banquet table. The speaker of the night is about to be introduced. The master of ceremonies steps to the microphone and says, "Before we hear from our guest tonight, I'd like to have a report from our social chairman." You are social chairman and it's a complete surprise. What you do is impromptu. Under the circumstances you might think that the methods of preparation we have discussed so far are irrelevant. You hardly have the time for the extensive preparation that I have been advocating. But you're wrong.

As you well know from your own listening experience, the worst thing an impromptu speaker can do is get up and just say something. The key to good impromptu speaking is pointedness and brevity. There is nothing worse than a speaker who is asked to say "a few words" and then says many words without ever really saying what he should have said. Pointless impromptu speeches are the easiest kind to give and if the speaker does not have an effective method of preparation, even under these circumstances he is likely to be hopelessly pointless.

The moment you are asked to speak your first step should be to formulate your central idea, even if you have to do it as you are walking to the microphone. As long as you have a central idea and can stick to it, you can't wander; you have avoided the greatest pitfall of impromptu speaking. Besides, once you have a clear central idea, your basic outline follows automatically. You can flesh out the speech while you are speaking.

Clearly this kind of instant preparation is not easy. It takes practice —not so much practice in impromptu speaking as practice in formulating clear central ideas. If you have made it a practice every time you have to make some sort of formal communication, whether written or spoken, first to formulate your central idea, then impromptu speaking will give you no difficulty at all.

The person who has developed this ability is easily recognized. Whenever he speaks, even in informal situations, he speaks to the point; he doesn't beat around the bush; he doesn't wander. He is easy to follow and speaks forcefully. When he argues, he knows precisely what the point at issue is. The person who has developed this ability is usually seen by others as clear-thinking and straightforward.

Extemporaneous

The next point of the continuum is extemporaneous speaking. This kind of speaking is prepared but it concentrates on the development of a good speech structure to which words are put at the time of delivery. Usually the speaker will bring notes along to the platform with him and will refer to them as he speaks. He has nothing written out and if he has notes at all they are usually key words to remind him of the basic outline he has prepared beforehand.

In preparing for this kind of speaking, the speaker should go through the steps of preparation discussed in this book. When he had completed the detailed outline, gathered all the necessary material, prepared or thought about his introduction and conclusion, and decided how each of his points fitted into the whole, he would then practice the speech. Practice would involve going over the speech and speaking it just as he would in the actual delivery. He would not be trying to memorize any particular pattern of words but rather trying out different patterns to see how effective they were.

As he went over his speech the speaker would rearrange, restructure, even rewrite parts of his detailed outline. His aim would always be to improve the structure of the speech. He would pay particular attention to the transitions and the way the speech hung together.

If the central idea was clearly worked out and if the structure was a good development of that central idea, the speaker will discover that he needs no notes at all or perhaps only a few notations containing any complex statistics or specific detailed examples. The more tightly logical the structure of the speech is, the easier it is to remember.

There are many advantages to this mode of delivery. The first is that it is hard to foul up. We tend to forget and stumble in a communication when we lose the connection of one thought to another. This becomes especially easy when we are concerned with words. In this form of delivery we are not concerned with particular words at all. What is in our mind at all times is the solid structure of the speech. If it has been well developed it is almost impossible to forget. The ancient Roman Cato put it very well: "Stick to your point, and the words will come by themselves."

The second advantage to the extemporaneous mode of delivery is that the speaker is free from notes or at least free from a dependence on them. He is free to observe his listener and respond to him. If the listener is not responding as the speaker wishes, the speaker is free enough to repeat, change the wording, emphasize differently, even restructure the speech itself.

A third advantage to the extemporaneous mode is that if a speaker is skilled in this kind of speaking, he will be skilled in any other mode as well. This kind of speaking forms the best basis for any other kind. This will become clear as we discuss the other modes of delivery.

Memorized

If you have heard speakers giving memorized speeches, you know what is usually wrong with them. When a speech has been memorized, the speaker often doesn't really seem to be speaking to you. It is as though he is reading a speech printed somewhere in his head and he doesn't have the time to pay attention to you. If he forgets a word, he falls apart. The speech usually sounds stiff and artificial; it strikes you as phony.

The reason is that the speaker is hung up on words and has lost the structure of his ideas. An actor memorizes his lines, but the good actor always knows precisely how the words fit into the sense of the whole play. If he forgets a word the structure of the whole recalls it for him or he can create new words to fit the sense. The structure, the sense, the idea of a message is what gives it life. The particular words make very little difference. If the idea comes through, the speech can never be a failure.

Therefore, if circumstances force you to memorize a speech, the preparation and practice should be no different from that of the extemporaneous speech. The point is to practice the speech extemporaneously until the words don't change anymore. At this point you have memorized the speech. A good memorized speech need never be written out, or if it must be written out it is the product of the speech, not the speech itself.

Most of us, when we write, tend to write essays not speeches. We use complex words, complex sentence structure, a great many abstractions. Even the best essays usually make poor speeches. If we write out a speech first and then memorize it, the likelihood is that it will be more an essay than a speech and it will not be very effective. If we prepare and practice as I suggest here, we can be sure that the speech will sound like a speech.

Manuscript

Under some circumstances it is necessary to write out a speech. Most papers at professional conventions are written. In situations where every word must be chosen with care, as when the Secretary of State is delivering a major foreign policy address, manuscript speaking is likely to be required. The same difficulties that we find in memorized speaking we encounter again in the manuscript mode of delivery. The difficulties are overcome in the same way.

If the speech must be written out, then it should be handled in precisely the same way as a memorized speech. The speaker should prepare his detailed outline as in extemporaneous speaking and then practice the speech in the same way. When he is satisfied with the way it sounds he may write it down.

In this way the speech at least will not be an essay. Moreover, the speaker will not be so bound to the manuscript that he cannot adapt it to changing situations while he is delivering it.

As a matter of fact, this procedure of preparation, except for the oral practice, is an effective way of preparing any formal written communication. It results in more unified, more tightly organized writing, particularly in expository or didactic writing.

Recorded Speech

The extreme end of this continuum of modes of delivery is the mechanically or electronically recorded speech, either auditory alone or audio-visual. Generally when a speech is taped for later playback the speech must be written, memorized, or so well practiced that there is little variation from one delivery of it to another. The hardest thing about recording a speech is that the speaker does not have the immediate feedback of audience response. One way to overcome this lack and to prevent the artificiality that often results is to record a presentation to live listeners. This is not too bad when the recording is of voice only, but TV recording does not adapt too well to live presentation. The reason is that the only contact with the television listener is through the lens of the camera. If the speaker spends time responding to the studio listener, he will tend to neglect the lens and therefore the TV listener.

Again, the most effective way to approach this situation is through the methods of preparation advised for the extemporaneous speech. This will leave the speaker free of a manuscript and able to concentrate on the camera lens. In recording a lecture or speech there is often need to interrupt the presentation and retake sections of it. If the speaker has memorized the words without paying attention enough to the structure of the speech, these interruptions are likely to be disconcerting to him and worse for the listener. The effect is even worse with a manuscript. With frequent interruption and attention to small parts of the speech, it becomes very easy to lose sight of the overall unit of the speech, and the result is a segmented, disconnected delivery. The best way to prevent these difficulties is to prepare for this type of speech just as you would for an extemporaneous speech.

COORDINATION OF DELIVERY AND THOUGHT

Whatever mode of delivery you choose, the most important element of your delivery will be its coordination with your idea. There is nothing that looks so false as a gesture that is clearly contrived. There is nothing that sounds so phony as a voice that doesn't match the sense of what is being said. There are no "little tricks" of delivery that can be used in every speech. The moment you consciously consider a gesture, or the moment you pay attention to the intonation of your voice, at that moment you have lost the purpose of your message. Gesture and voice that do not grow naturally out of the sense of what you are saying will inevitably destroy the message. When you are delivering your speech you should be thinking about only one thing—getting your idea across.

How then do you improve gestures and voice? Your first concern should always be the structure of your speech. This should be your main job even when you have completed the detailed outline and are practicing. Even in practice you should be striving to improve the structure of your ideas. But during your practice is the time to develop your use of voice and your movements. As you are fitting words to your outline try out new and different gestures, variations of intonation and rate. In fact, in practice, you should overdo concern for gesture and voice. Let yourself be as extreme and artificial as you wish. The time to experiment with this sort of thing is in practice, not when you are talking to your listener. Then, when you face your listener, let your only concern be your idea and the listener's response. The gestures and the voice will come. As Cato said: *rem tene; verba sequentur.*

SUMMARY

The best form of preparation, no matter what mode of delivery the speaker uses, is that which concentrates on the structure of ideas, the main concern of this book.

Exercises

1. Develop a complete speech for this class.
2. Indicate in writing how you would change it for each mode of delivery discussed in this chapter.
3. Select two modes and present one mode to one-half of the class and the other mode to the other half.
4. After delivery compare the two and indicate how you should have adapted the speech to each mode.

Chapter 9

CONTENT AND ETHICS

We began this book with the statement that all formal public speaking is persuasive in nature. Whether conscious or not, whether intended or not, the aim of the speaker is to change the listener in some specific way. From the beginning we have insisted that it is not the speaker's predilections that determine what points are covered in a speech, what order they are to be dealt with, what material is used to support them, but rather it is the listener who determines. If it is the aim of the speaker to change the listener, and since it is the listener's choice whether to be changed or not, it is therefore the demands of the listener that determine all aspects of content and organization.

You will remember, however, that I said the speaker is given a position of potential influence when he is allowed to speak to a group. I said that this position of influence brings with it a responsibility. It is necessary at this point to examine that responsibility.

THE NATURE OF CHOICE

Most of us like to think that our choices are rational. Admittedly, our rationality is often mere rationalization. We know that often our "emotions" drive us to make a choice and then after we have chosen what we really desire, we make up a plausible logical reason for our actions. Some of us might even be honest enough to say that a great many of our decisions are made in this way.

Let's examine the choice to smoke or not to smoke. After the Surgeon General's report on the relationship between lung cancer, heart diseases, and smoking, there has not been much factual dispute about whether or not smoking is harmful to health. Most people have accepted what they feel is an inevitable conclusion. To be sure, there are some who still dispute the existence of that relationship: some tobacco companies and their satellite scientific researchers, even some smokers who have no claim to scientific expertise. Most of us would say that people who argue that a link between lung cancer and smoking either does not exist or has not been proved are biased advocates who have let their personal interests interfere with their reason. These people certainly are not making a rational choice.

What about that large majority of smokers who believe that smoking is harmful to their health but continue to smoke anyway? True, most of them have probably switched to a filter brand, but these people would be the first to admit that filters probably do not remove the threat to their health. They know smoking is harmful but they consciously choose to smoke anyway. They have weighed the value of health in a hopefully distant future against the present pleasures of continued smoking. Clearly such a decision is based on a hierarchy of values, values which, however good and proper, are based not upon reason but upon some nonrational or irrational process. The sources of these values are often not only non-rational but are likely to be unconscious. Perhaps the value working here is an unconscious identification with a father who smoked. Perhaps it is a rebellion against an authority figure who frowns on smoking. Perhaps it may even be an unconscious death wish. Whatever the value, its source is beyond reason.

But what about the person who decides not to smoke? Until the time he became convinced that smoking was a hazard, he smoked heavily. Then when the clear logic of the Surgeon General's report got through to him he simply stopped smoking. Here was a man who was led by reason.

Was he really led by logic? I think not. Here too the choice was made by weighing one value against another. Perhaps he stopped smoking because he was afraid of getting lung cancer. Fear cannot be considered a rational motive. Whatever the value that led him to make the choice to quit smoking, it was a value and values are not rationally derived.

But even if the actual choice to give up the habit was not rational, at least the act of believing the truth of the Surgeon General's report was rational. Through the rational methods of statistics the report proved beyond any doubt that smoking increased one's chances of contracting lung cancer or heart disease. Belief in that fact was certainly rational.

In most cases belief was certainly not rational. Most people who believed in the report did so because of its source. The Surgeon General was a reputable, trustworthy source. These people were motivated by the value they placed upon an authority figure, or on the institution of which he was a part. Others believed because of the sheer complexity of the statistical method used—not because the method was a good one, but only because it seemed so scientific. Clearly this was no rational motive for belief.

Finally, the person who believes the report because of its scientific rigor certainly seems the most objective of all. But he too is making his choice by a nonrational commitment to a value. He places a value on scientific rigor.

Whatever the choice it is a matter of value; the act of choice is a nonrational act. The effect is that you risk yourself because you trust. This is inevitable and ultimately it is good because this is how we learn.

A LOOK AT LEARNING

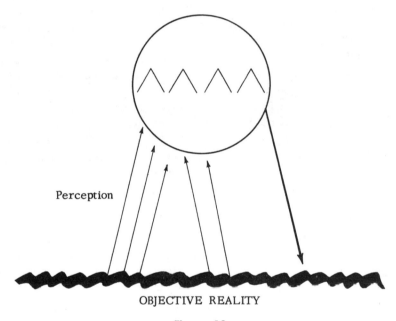

Perception

OBJECTIVE REALITY

Figure 13

In the diagram above, the wavy line at the bottom represents whatever objective reality really is. We know that it is in process, undergoing constant change. We know that we cannot know or understand all of it. We do, however, receive some energy transfers from that reality and to some of them our sense organs respond. When they arrive at those end organs we can say that we have received some sort of information from our reality. The circle represents our cognitive and organizational functions; it represents what we do with this incoming information. From our previous discussion in Chapter 6 we know that the organization, the structure of what we perceive as our reality is much different from that reality itself. We know that what we do with that information is wholly symbolic in nature. Thus in our cognition and organizational system we arrange, give structure to, this incoming data. We formulate symbolic concepts and concept systems that constitute satisfying explanations of what we perceive. These concept systems are what we use to organize our behavior. They are hypotheses about what reality is, what we are, how reality and we are related, and hypotheses about the consequences of particular and generalized behavior patterns.

We then make choices, represented by the arrow on the right. In effect we predict the consequence of any particular choice and we evaluate that predicted consequence. If the value we place on it is sufficiently high, we choose: to perceive, to believe, to trust, to speak, to act. No matter how accurate our data gathering systems are, no matter how carefully our concept systems have worked to formulate accurate reality concepts, and no matter how reasonably we have measured out the consequences, the act of choice is always a risk.

But note what happens. When we choose, we commit ourselves to a test of our information and our concepts. If, after we have chosen, the new information that we continually gather confirms our original choice, our confidence in that choice increases. If it is infirmed by the new information, our confidence is shaken and we begin to gather more data and to reformulate our concepts until we have established a more satisfactory concept. We then risk another choice.

In short, we cannot really learn without risking. In fact, we cannot really learn unless all parts of this system operate efficiently: unless we are free to gather information, free to formulate and reformulate our concepts, and free to make choices.

If we interfere with this process in any way, we are thereby hindering the learning process of the individual, we are preventing the growth of the person. We can therefore postulate a value system. If we value the learning and growth of people, then those people have three absolute rights. Those rights are the right to gather all the information they need to form concepts about themselves and their world, the right to formulate any concept that they need to make sense out of their information and deal with their world, and the right to choose how to express their concepts verbally or in behavior. There follows from this a set of ethical principles that we are obliged to respect, if we value the human individual.

Freedom of Information

No speaker has the right to knowingly distort or limit information that a person needs to make appropriate choices in his behavior. If the manufacturer of a child's toy advertises it as educational and fun, but fails to say it is highly inflammable, he is withholding information necessary to an appropriate choice. By these standards he is acting immorally. Whenever a speaker limits or distorts information knowingly for the purpose of getting a listener to respond favorably he is committing an immoral act.

Freedom of Conceptualization

No speaker has the right to manipulate or attempt to manipulate the concepts a person forms by any other means than pointing out the alternatives of a choice. To knowingly limit the alternatives a person has violates his freedom.

You might ask how a speaker can limit the choice of a listener. In Chapter 3 we talked about the process of identification. There we recognized the fact that people respond to the alternatives of a choice not just because they place a value on the consequences of that alternative, but also because that alternative is associated in that person's mind with a person, object, or idea with which the person identifies. That is, regardless of the real consequences of a choice, and regardless of the values the individual himself places on those consequences, he can be made to choose because someone he trusts or respects so chooses.

Let me indicate what follows from our discussion of learning and the freedom of conceptualization. It seems to follow that a speaker can argue the consequences of a choice. He can argue that a particular consequence of a choice is to be valued. But he may not knowingly lead me to make that choice *because* it is associated with something with which I identify, or *because* the opposite choice is associated with something with which I disidentify. Anything then which limits, or forces my acceptance of a concept, or makes me accept that concept on irrational grounds, is immoral.

Freedom of Choice

The only way a person has of testing his concepts is by putting them to use in the real world. This means that the individual must be free to choose his behavior. Now, wait a minute! What about the laws? Well, ultimately even here the individual should be free to act with society or against it. Then if that society does not like the individual's *behavior* it has some right (and maybe even duty) to punish *some* behaviors. But the human being should still have the right to give some test to his concepts, even the most violently antisocial. The ability to express his concepts verbally gives him his opportunity to test. Limit a person's behavior, but do not limit his right to speak in any way.

The person then should have the right to gather information, to conceptualize, and to choose and express his choices. No speaker has the right to violate these rights, for to do so is to damage that person's right to learn and grow.

This seems to me a reasonable ethic for the speaker or for anyone else. Whether you will accept it or reject it is your choice. Elsewhere in this book we talked of the position of potential power the speaker has. How you use that power is up to you.

Immanuel Kant put his ethic into two magnificent postulates. Treat other people as ends in themselves and not as means to your ends. Act in such a way that you would be happy to have the principle of your action applied by everyone. I think those two postulates epitomize what I have to say.

EXERCISES

1. Develop your own theory of an ethic of communication or persuasion.
2. Argue it before the class.

READINGS

On the theory of learning presented in this chapter see:

> BRONOWSKI, J., *Science and Human Values* (New York: Harper and Row), 1965.
> (This book is a simpler treatment of the ideas of Ernst Cassirer in such sources as the essay *Einstein's Theory of Relativity,* his *Essay on Man,* and his three-volume *Philosophy of Symbolic Form.*)

For another alternative on an ethic of communication see the final chapter of:

> MINNICK, WAYNE C., *The Art of Persuasion* (Boston: Houghton Mifflin Company, 1957), pp. 276-287.

INDEX